GREEK SOPHISTS
IN THE
ROMAN EMPIRE

G. W. BOWERSOCK

PROFESSOR OF GREEK AND LATIN
HARVARD UNIVERSITY

OXFORD
AT THE CLARENDON PRESS
1969

Oxford University Press, Ely House, London W. 1

GLASGOW NEW YORK TORONTO MELBOURNE WELLINGTON
CAPE TOWN SALISBURY IBADAN NAIROBI LUSAKA ADDIS ABABA
BOMBAY CALCUTTA MADRAS KARACHI LAHORE DACCA
KUALA LUMPUR SINGAPORE HONG KONG TOKYO

© OXFORD UNIVERSITY PRESS 1969

PRINTED IN GREAT BRITAIN

PREFACE

ABUNDANT scholarly inquiries have, in the past, been conse-
crated to studies of the so-called Second Sophistic as an
aspect of Greek Literature, but little attention has so far
been directed to placing the sophistic movement as a whole
within the history of the Roman empire. The present book is
intended to correct this situation. The limits of discussion are,
in general, those provided by Philostratus' *Lives of the Sophists*.
The subject might have been expanded indefinitely: there is
no shortage of evidence for the period, and—as will be seen—
study of the sophists leads straight into central problems of
imperial history. There might, further, have been a parallel
and no less detailed account of the roles of other literary personalities. But every effort has been made to confine these
matters so as not to obscure the principal theme. The final
chapter exists solely to set in perspective what has gone
before.

The entire book takes its origin from a series of lectures on
'Sophists and the Roman Government in the Second Century
A.D.', delivered at Oxford University under the Faculty of
Literae Humaniores in Michaelmas Term, 1966. I am much
indebted to the faithful auditors of those lectures for comments
and friendly encouragement. Various parts of this work were
also presented independently as lectures in Liverpool, Leeds,
London, Toronto, and Philadelphia; and I am grateful too for
helpful criticism in those centres of learning. In studying the
second and early third centuries I have always profited from
lively controversy with Dr. Charles Behr, and I have once
again to record the unflagging and unselfish aid of Professor
C. P. Jones. Further, I have to thank Dr. Richard Walzer
and T. D. Barnes for generous counsel. My historical approach
to the Greek renaissance of the Roman empire has been long

in evolution and illustrates the development of one of the major topics in *Augustus and the Greek World* (1965). Throughout all my studies of Rome and the East Professor Syme has taken so constant an interest that I cannot adequately express my appreciation.

G. W. B.

Harvard University
October, 1968

CONTENTS

ABBREVIATIONS

AE	*L'Année épigraphique*
AJA	*American Journal of Archaeology*
AJP	*American Journal of Philology*
Ant. Class.	*L'Antiquité classique*
Ath. Mitt.	*Mitteilungen des deutschen archäologischen Instituts, Athenische Abteilung*
BCH	*Bulletin de correspondance hellénique*
CIG	*Corpus Inscriptionum Graecarum*
CIL	*Corpus Inscriptionum Latinarum*
CP	*Classical Philology*
CQ	*Classical Quarterly*
CR	*Classical Review*
FGH	F. Jacoby, *Die Fragmente der griechischen Historiker*
GRBS	*Greek, Roman, and Byzantine Studies*
HA	*Historia Augusta*
HSCP	*Harvard Studies in Classical Philology*
IG	*Inscriptiones Graecae*
IGR	*Inscriptiones Graecae ad Res Romanas Pertinentes*
ILS	H. Dessau, *Inscriptiones Latinae Selectae*
JHS	*Journal of Hellenic Studies*
JÖAI	*Jahreshefte des österreichischen archäologischen Instituts*
JRS	*Journal of Roman Studies*
JTS	*Journal of Theological Studies*
MAMA	*Monumenta Asiae Minoris Antiqua*
NGA	*Nachrichten der Akademie der Wissenschaften in Göttingen*, Phil.-Hist. Klasse
OGIS	*Orientis Graeci Inscriptiones Selectae*
PIR	*Prosopographia Imperii Romani* (*PIR²* referring to available volumes of the Second Edition)
P–W	Pauly–Wissowa–Kroll, *Real-Encyclopädie*
REA	*Revue des études anciennes*
REG	*Revue des études grecques*
REL	*Revue des études latines*
Rh. Mus.	*Rheinisches Museum*

SEG	*Supplementum Epigraphicum Graecum*
SIG[3]	W. Dittenberger, *Sylloge Inscriptionum Graecarum* (Third Edition)
TAPA	*Transactions of the American Philological Association*
VS	Philostratus, *Vitae Sophistarum* (with reference to the Olearius pagination)

All other abbreviations should be clear enough without further expansion.

I

THE BIOGRAPHER OF THE
SOPHISTS

LITERATURE, illuminating the society of an age through
acquiescence or dissent, must always have its place in
history as a reflection of attitudes and taste. The relation
of literature to politics, however, has not been uniform throughout the ages; from time to time there have developed close
alliances between literature and politics,—in England, for
example, in the early eighteenth century. Similarly, in the
second century of the present era, literary men helped to
determine the destiny of the Roman empire and never enjoyed
more public renown. Their social and political eminence was
not necessarily matched by superior literary attainments. The
quality of the second-century works we possess (and they
are many) is not high:[1] they are often over-elaborated pro-
ductions on unreal, unimportant, or traditional themes. Such
works were rhetorical showpieces, whose authors, highly
trained in oral presentation, were showmen. Yet this fact does
not preclude composition for important persons and occasions.
The authors were themselves important men.

These were the sophists, still better known (where they are
known at all) to philologists than to historians. They are
crucial for the history of the second century A.D., which would
look far different without them. Their enormous popularity
and influence is characteristic of that exquisitely refined epoch;
and their extensive travels, with numerous friends in diverse
cities, illustrate a coherence of the Roman empire that had
been long in the making and was not to exist again. Authors
like Lucian and Aelius Aristides brilliantly mirror the world in
which the sophists flourished.

From the writings of the second century alone it would have

[1] B. A. van Groningen, 'General Literary Tendencies in the Second Century
A.D.', *Mnemosyne* 18 (1965), 41 ff.

been possible to construct an adequate account of the sophists. In addition, the plentiful evidence of inscriptions and papyri reveals a staggering abundance of practitioners of the sophistic arts. From all this material alone favourite subjects of discourse and standard treatments of them can be adequately established; so can certain details of the sophists' petty quarrels. But, by some good fortune, Flavius Philostratus, a sophist born in the second century and dying in the third, composed the lives of many of his distinguished predecessors and near-contemporaries; his work has survived and provides a convenient basis and limit for historical studies of the movement which he himself designated the Second Sophistic (to detach it from the age of Gorgias). Inasmuch as Philostratus exemplifies what he is writing about and is at the same time so important a source, discussion of the man and the whole notion of a 'sophistic' is inevitable.

The family of Philostratus is a notorious snare. A late Greek lexicon registers three sophists with the name Philostratus,[1] and the confusion generated by these items has long frustrated scholarly certitude.[2] The first man to be listed belongs second chronologically: he is manifestly the biographer of the sophists. The *Lives of the Sophists* and the romantic biography of Apollonius of Tyana are numbered among his works. The conjunction is supported by a reference in the *Lives* back to the account of Apollonius, which is automatically established as the earlier of the two works.[3]

While it is agreeable to recognize one of the Philostrati in the lexicographer's trio, the pleasure is spoiled by obscurities in the two other items. The biographer is said to have flourished under Septimius Severus and to have survived until the reign of Philip the Arab. Those chronological indications are approximately correct.[4] Yet this Philostratus is credited with an

---

[1] Suid., s.v. Φιλόστρατος, nos. 421–3 (Adler).
[2] Cf. the survey in F. Solmsen, 'Philostratus', *P–W* 20. 1. 125 ff. and Solmsen, 'Some Works of Philostratus the Elder', *TAPA* 71 (1940), 556 ff.
[3] *VS*, p. 570: εἴρηται σαφῶς ἐν τοῖς ἐς Ἀπολλώνιον.
[4] Suid., s.v. Φιλόστρατος, no. 421 (Adler): ἐπὶ Σευήρου τοῦ βασιλέως καὶ ἕως Φιλίππου. The Severus is Septimius (cf. Rohde, *Rh. Mus* 33 [1878], 638–9). For the accuracy of this rough chronology, see the discussion of Philostratus' career later in the present chapter.

eminent father who practised the sophistic arts under Nero.[1] Something has gone wrong; hence an inclination on the part of scholars to see pure fiction in the report of the biographer's famous father. However, there may be truth in it up to a point. The man is said to have composed a work entitled *Nero*; whatever that work may have been, it is just the sort of thing that would induce a lexicographer like this one to lodge the author in Nero's reign. The biographer's father ought to have flourished under the Antonines. Three of the writings attributed to the father can be assigned precisely to that period: a letter to the sophist Antipater, a *Proteus*, and the *Nero* itself. Antipater was one of the biographer's teachers and would plausibly have belonged to his father's generation.[2] Proteus was a name of the notorious Cynic of whom Lucian composed a satiric biography —Peregrinus Proteus, who immolated himself at Olympia in 165.[3] No less a theme for a Philostratus than for a Lucian.[4] Finally, the *Nero* calls swiftly to mind the dialogue now extant in the corpus of Lucian, *Nero or Digging Through the Isthmus of Corinth*. Whether this work, associated falsely with Lucian, is or is not the Philostratean *Nero*, it directs attention to Nero's great scheme to put through a canal from the Corinthian to the Saronic Gulf.[5] That was a matter of relevance in the Antonine age, for the sophist Herodes Atticus contemplated the same plan but was deterred by the ominous example of the emperor Nero.[6] It seems best to allow a historical existence to the eldest Philostratus and to leave him with the works assigned to him. All the chronological indications cohere, apart from one that is wholly impossible (but easily explicable). There is insufficient warrant to remove the man altogether and to ascribe his writings to his son.[7]

---

[1] Suid., s.v. Φιλόστρατος, no. 422 (Adler).　　[2] See below pp. 55–6.

[3] Lucian, *Peregrinus*: the immolation is described in ch. 36 (cf. *VS*, p. 563, Amm. Marc. 29. 1. 39). On the date of the event: K. von Fritz, *P–W* 19. 1. 657 and G. Bagnani, *Historia* 4 (1955), 108.

[4] Suidas also ascribes to this Philostratus a work entitled τὰ ἐν 'Ολυμπίᾳ ἐπιτελούμενα. Perhaps including an account of Peregrinus' immolation?

[5] On Nero's plan, see Dio 62. 16. 1–2.　　　　[6] *VS*, pp. 551–2.

[7] It is true that Philostratus does not mention his father at all (cf. F. Grosso, *Acme* 7 [1954], 376 n. 23). Should he? Plutarch says relatively little, in all his vast writings, about his father. As a sophist, the biographer's father may have had no importance.

The case of the third Philostratus is hopeless. The lexicon blandly states that he was a grand-nephew and a son-in-law of the biographer.[1] He is said to have composed a set of word pictures, and indeed the biographer is also credited with a similar production. Curiously there survive under the name of a Philostratus one set of *imagines* and under the name of 'Philostratus the Younger' another set. But if the latter *imagines* are associated with the third Philostratus in the lexicon, that man emerges (from an avowal in the opening paragraph of the set) as a grandson of the biographer.[2] This is too much to believe, in addition to everything else. It is more judicious to create a fourth Philostratus, author of the second set of *imagines*; it is probably best to remain baffled.

The biographer Philostratus, it seems, came from Lemnos.[3] If his father was a sophist, it should not be surprising, since often in the high empire the profession descended within a family.[4] There were years of study at Athens.[5] In the course of the *Lives* Philostratus mentions several men as his teachers, including Proclus of Naucratis and Hippodromus of Larissa, both themselves taught by pupils of the great Herodes Atticus.[6] Philostratus also names among his teachers the celebrated Damian of Ephesus and Antipater from Phrygian Hierapolis (to whom his father may have addressed a letter).[7] The last of these was instructor of the sons of Septimius Severus. It cannot

[1] Suid., s.v. Φιλόστρατος, no. 423 (Adler).

[2] On all this, see Solmsen, *TAPA* 71 (1940), 556 ff.

[3] Eunapius, *Vit. Phil. et Soph.*, p. 454 (ὁ Λήμνιος, of the biographer of sophists); Synesius, *Dio* 1; Suid., s.v. Apollonius Tyaneus and s.v. Crates Cynicus. Cf. Schmid, *Philol.* 57 (1898), 503. Note Philostratus' reference to Lemnos in *Vit. Apoll.* 6. 27 and his allusion to a younger contemporary (and, presumably, relative), Philostratus of Lemnos, at *VS*, p. 617. Cf. Philostr. *Epist.* 70.

[4] Observe, e.g., the Licinii Firmi of Athens (*IG* ii/iii². 3563, cf. *Anth. Plan.* 322), the Flavii Menandri of Ephesus (*Forsch. Ephesos* 3. 145, no. 62), the Claudii Aurelii of Aphrodisias (L. Robert, *Ant. Class.* 35 [1966], 396–7), the Flavii Alexander, Phylax, and Phoenix of Thessaly (*PIR*², F 199; cf. J. Pouilloux, *REG* 80 [1967], 379 ff.).

[5] Suid., s.v. Φιλόστρατος, no. 421 (Adler). Eusebius and Hierocles called him an Athenian (*PIR*², F 332). Philostratus will have heard Proclus and Hippodromus in Athens. See next note.

[6] *VS*, pp. 602 (Proclus), 618 (Hippodromus).

[7] *VS*, pp. 605–6 (Damian), 607 (Antipater). On the letter to Antipater, see the foregoing discussion in this chapter.

be said whether Philostratus studied with Antipater at Rome or elsewhere;[1] since, however, Philostratus belonged to the circle of the Syrian empress, Julia Domna, he may well have been introduced to it by Antipater himself.[2] From early in the third century, in all probability, Philostratus mingled with the luminaries of the empress and travelled with them in the great lady's entourage. The opening of the Lives of the Sophists records a conversation conducted with a certain Gordian, perhaps a member of the group, in a suburb of Syrian Antioch. It was in Antioch precisely that Julia Domna received word in 217 of Caracalla's death and thereupon took her own life.[3]

Philostratus was at the time engaged in the composition of his Apollonius novel, undertaken at the behest of Julia Domna but completed, or at any rate published, only after her death.[4] It is impossible to say how long it was after her suicide before the work appeared: perhaps not too long, or the reference to Julia's influence might have been less interesting. In any case, Philostratus' allusion to the Apollonius novel in the Lives establishes that they at least were written after it.

A juxtaposition of several items compels an inference that the sophists' biographies were done in Athens. A lexicographical entry concerned with one Fronto of Emesa records that Philostratus was teaching in Athens at the same time as Apsines of Gadara, and we happen to know from the biographer himself that Apsines was a younger contemporary and friend of his.[5] Therefore, Philostratus will have found himself in

---

[1] In P-W 20. 1. 136, Solmsen objected rightly to a terminus ante of 193 for Philostratus' study with Antipater: this terminus was postulated by K. Münscher in Philol. Supp. 10 (1905-7), 475-6, on the unsupported assumption that Philostratus heard Antipater at Athens. VS, p. 607 tells how Philostratus used to praise Antipater's lectures at Rome.

[2] On Philostratus' membership in Julia's circle, Vit. Apoll. 1. 3: μετέχοντι δέ μοι τοῦ περὶ αὐτὴν κύκλου.

[3] VS, p. 480 (the conversation outside Antioch). On the suicide of Julia: Dio 79. 23-4.

[4] The work is not dedicated to Julia, although Philostratus states explicitly that he wrote it at her instigation (Vit. Apoll. 1. 3).

[5] Suid., s.v. Φρόντων ’Εμισηνός: the biographer is called, in this entry, ὁ πρῶτος (cf. W. Schmid, Der Atticismus [1896], p. 6 with n. 6). See also VS, p. 628. An Athenian inscription now provides the nomen Valerius for Apsines and links him with an important family of Athens, the Claudii of Melite: Hesperia 10 (1941), 261.

Athens with Apsines in the later years of his career and formed then the association which he attests at the end of the *Lives*. Furthermore, an inscription at Olympia alludes clearly to the biographer Flavius Philostratus and calls him Athenian.[1] In view of Philostratus' presence at the court for many years, there seems little doubt that the residence in Athens implied by these items followed Julia Domna's suicide.

A text from Erythrae must not be forgotten here: it displays senatorial descendants of Flavius Philostratus 'the sophist', and his wife, a certain Aurelia Melitine.[2] The progression from sophist to senator in successive generations was not uncommon in this age. Examples abound from the second and third centuries.[3]

The dedication of the *Lives of the Sophists* has a peculiar interest. The recipient is Antonius Gordianus ὁ λαμπρότατος ὕπατος; at the end of the dedicatory preface he is addressed as ἄριστε ἀνθυπάτων. Who is this Gordian, and what is the date of the dedication? Standard and accessible works declare that the forms of address indicate that this is Gordian I, at the time proconsul of Africa,[4]—a post he was definitely holding when he became in 238 the first emperor of that name.[5] In the Augustan History Gordian I is said to have held two consulates, the second with Severus Alexander: allegedly in 229.[6] On this uncertain evidence a date of 229/30 has long been considered the *terminus post* for the *Lives*, with Gordian's elevation to the Purple as the *terminus ante*.[7] These *termini* presuppose a possibility which is altogether inadmissible: that Gordian could have gone to the proconsulate of Africa directly after his consulate and stayed there until he became emperor.

---

[1] *SIG*³ 878: Φλ. Φιλόστρατον Ἀθηναῖον τὸν σοφιστήν.

[2] *SIG*³ 879 = *IGR* 4. 1544.

[3] Many illustrations of this progression will be found in the pages that follow.

[4] e.g. Münscher, op. cit. (p. 5, n. 1), p. 471, or Solmsen, *P–W* 20. 1. 138 and 170.

[5] *HA* Tres Gordiani 2. 4, 5. 1, 7. 2, 18. 6. Cf. B. E. Thomasson, *Die Statthalter der römischen Provinzen Nordafrikas von Augustus bis Diokletianus* (1960), pp. 120–1.

[6] *HA* Tres Gordiani 2. 4, 4. 1. Alexander Severus was *consul ordinarius* III in 229 with Cassius Dio, *cos. ord.* II; it would have to be assumed that a suffect replaced Dio while the emperor remained in office. Alexander was also *cos. ord.* in 222 and 226.

[7] Cf. *PIR*², A 833.

Objections can and have been raised against such an assumption. There is no warrant for believing in a second consulate for Gordian or that he held the African proconsulate for longer than a year. Moreover, Philostratus will have addressed Gordian at the outset by his highest and most recent office, while at the same time acknowledging him to have been an excellent proconsul of a province not specified. The consulate was thus Gordian's most recent office (Philostratus' ὕπατος need mean no more than ὑπατικός) ;[1] the proconsulate was praetorian, not consular. This conclusion furnishes an explanation for the absence of a province's name in connection with the proconsulate: it was the praetorian proconsulate of Achaea, the province in which Philostratus was living.[2] Accordingly, the old chronological *termini* for the *Lives of the Sophists* vanish. The work was composed some time after the year of Gordian's only consulate, a year regrettably unknown.

There is, however, another possibility, recently propounded.[3] Perhaps Gordian II, not I, is the recipient of Philostratus' work. In his preface Philostratus states that his Gordian was descended from Herodes Atticus,[4]—on any hypothesis an exceedingly difficult detail to elucidate. One is reluctant to doubt the connection with Herodes; Philostratus' account of that sophist is certainly the longest of any and prominently placed at the opening of the second book of the *Lives*. The second Gordian is more easily traced back to Herodes than the first,[5] but in neither case is the evidence sufficient. Credibility

[1] For Philostratus' usage, observe the following instances where ὕπατος means 'consular' (ὑπατικός): p. 512 (ἀνὴρ ὕπατος), p. 536 (τοῦ ὕπατός τε καὶ ἐξ ὑπάτων δοκεῖν), p. 555 (ἐν ὑπάτοις), p. 567 (ἐς ὑπάτους), p. 576 (Κοδρατίων ὁ ὕπατος), p. 588 (ἀνδρὸς ὑπάτου), p. 609 (ἀνὴρ ὕπατος). Scholars have attended insufficiently to this usage in Philostratus. It is not unlike the word *consul* on a cursus inscription well after a man has ceased actually being consul.

[2] Cf. E. Groag, *Die römischen Reichsbeamten von Achaia von Augustus bis auf Diokletian* (1939), 87–8. Philostratus was writing after 222: *VS*, pp. 624–5.

[3] A. R. Birley, *Britain and Rome: Essays pres. to E. Birley* (1966), pp. 58–9. For a full discussion of this possibility: T. D. Barnes, 'Philostratus and Gordian', *Latomus* 27 (1968), 581 ff.

[4] *VS*, p. 479: γένος ἐστί σοι πρὸς τὴν τέχνην ἐς Ἡρώδην τὸν σοφιστὴν ἀναφέροντι. For the view that Philostratus errs here, cf. J. H. Oliver, *AJP* 89 (1968), 346.

[5] Since Gordian I was about eighty years old when he became emperor in 238 (Herodian 7. 5. 2; *HA* Tres Gord. 9. 1), he was born *c.* 159. Of Herodes' two daughters it is hard to see which could have been Gordian's mother,

does not permit belief that Gordian I was the author of an epic poem in thirty books on the exploits of Pius and Marcus, as the Augustan History avers;[1] but it is not impossible that he was a man of literary tastes whom Philostratus may have known in the salon of Julia Domna. Until more evidence or argument accrues, Gordian I has a slightly superior claim as the honorand of Philostratus.

The Gordiani probably came from Asia Minor.[2] It is an instructive spectacle to see the sophist Philostratus presenting a work on sophists to an East Greek, soon to be emperor, whom he may have known at an earlier time in the Roman salon of a Syrian empress and whom he had encountered more recently as governor of the Greeks in Achaea. This is a fitting illustration of the historical significance of the so-called Second Sophistic.

Philostratus himself insisted upon the term 'Second Sophistic' for the efflorescence of sophists under the Roman empire. One ought not, he said, to call it the 'New Sophistic' (which evokes a suspicion that someone had), since it was old.[3] It began, according to Philostratus, with Aeschines, the great rival of Demosthenes.[4] Gorgias is credited with an older type of sophistic which concerned itself with philosophical themes, such as justice and the universe, treated rhetorically; it was 'philosophic rhetoric'.[5] The second form of the sophistic art, rightly or wrongly traced to Aeschines, is characterized by historical themes or at any rate types of persons who figure in history (princes, dynasts, the rich, the poor). Philostratus' rather arbitrary distinction would disqualify the prose hymns of Aristides; but, after all, these were quite self-consciously new contributions to sophistic literature.[6] The definition of Philostratus is serviceable enough; as for the antiquity claimed

although Elpinice, dying after Athenaïs and without recorded husband, is possible (cf. *PIR²*, C 802). However, Claudia Regilla, wife of M. Antonius Lupus, might be exploited as mother of Gordian II in a previous marriage (she predeceased Lupus, cf. *ILS* 1127). The name Claudia Regilla proclaims some connection with Herodes and his wife Regilla.

[1] *HA* Tres Gordiani 3. 3.
[2] A. R. Birley, op. cit. (p. 7, n. 3), pp. 59–60, and the opinion of H.-G. Pflaum cited by Birley.   [3] *VS*, p. 481.
[4] Ibid., p. 507.   [5] Ibid., p. 480: ῥητορικὴ φιλοσοφοῦσα.
[6] Cf. Aristid. 45. 4–14 Keil (Hymn to Serapis) on the writing of prose hymns.

for the movement by allusion to Aeschines, even Philostratus is hard put to think of any other representatives after Aeschines before the reign of Nero.[1] He mentions exactly three names from that vast intervening period and dismisses them immediately with a reference to the paucity of noble sophists in those times.[2] The plain fact is that the Second Sophistic, whether it might have derived from Aeschines or not, was a distinctive growth of the high empire, and it would not have been a senseless man who called it new.

It was, however, a growth, and there were certainly sophists before Nicetes of Smyrna, whose biography follows directly upon that of Aeschines in Philostratus. Cicero and Strabo leave no doubt of the activity of sophists and rhetors in the late republic and early empire; the reminiscences of the elder Seneca convey a similar impression.[3] Moreover, these earlier figures often had careers in politics and diplomacy: so, for example, Hybreas of Mylasa and the Augustan Polemo.[4] And as Polemo's family makes clear in subsequent generations,[5] there are palpable links between these earlier cultivated men and the true representatives of the Second Sophistic. There is continuity and development throughout, so much so that the Second Sophistic would not have occurred, had the way not been prepared. The Second (or New) Sophistic is a culmination, not a sudden burst or fad. This is true of the sophists' style as much as it is of their role in Roman history.

In the late nineteenth century the question of style in the Second Sophistic was hotly debated by the scholarly giants of the day. In retrospect the whole argument has an air of absurdity. It began when Erwin Rohde devoted a division of his thick book on the Greek novel to detailing the spread of

---

[1] *VS*, p. 511, Nicetes of Smyrna. He has to be dated to the reign of Nero: the emperor on p. 512 is not Nerva but Nero (cf. A. Boulanger, *Aelius Aristide* [1923], p. 84, n. 1).

[2] The three (all unknown) are Ariobarzanes of Cilicia, Xenophron of Sicily, and Peithagoras of Cyrene (*VS*, p. 511).

[3] U. von Wilamowitz, *Litteris* 2 (1925), 127. Cf. Bowersock, *Augustus and the Greek World* (1965), ch. 1. For Strabo, there is the very useful book of E. Stemplinger, *Strabons literarhistorische Notizen* (1894); for Seneca some of the persons in H. Bornecque's register are relevant: *Les déclamations et les déclamateurs d'après Sénèque le père* (1902).

[4] Bowersock, op. cit., pp. 5–6.   [5] Ibid., pp. 143–4.

Asianic rhetoric so as to demonstrate that the second century saw nothing more than a perpetuation of the Asianic style of Cicero's era.[1] Kaibel denied this, and he summoned as witnesses the Atticists among the sophists;[2] Rohde replied.[3] Norden observed sanely that the Second Sophistic had both Atticist *and* Asianic manifestations.[4] Wilamowitz finally closed the case by synthesizing everyone's views in a long and important article.[5]

Continuity, one has always to realize, does not require sameness; and an opposite reaction can nevertheless belong to a single line of development. The Second Sophistic is distinguishable and new not because it introduced a new type of person into literature and history, but rather because in the second century a type, long in existence, became so widely diffused and enjoyed such unprecedented authority. An access of inscriptions and papyri, enlarging our knowledge of social and political history, has authoritatively vindicated Philostratus' recognition of a great sophistic movement. The notion, once fashionable among scholars, that the Second Sophistic was a pure invention of its chronicler has to be banished.[6] Philostratus was not a scholar himself and his work is often superficial, but his subject was a real one.

In the work presented to Gordian Philostratus claimed to be writing biographies not only of true sophists (τοὺς οὕτω κυρίως προσρηθέντας σοφιστάς) but also of philosophers who could be regarded as sophists (τοὺς φιλοσοφήσαντας ἐν δόξῃ τοῦ σοφιστεῦσαι).[7] A little later Philostratus alludes to those philosophers

---

[1] E. Rohde, *Der griechische Roman* (1914), pp. 310–87. This material appeared in the first edition of 1876.

[2] G. Kaibel, 'Dionysios von Halikarnassos und die Sophistik', *Hermes* 20 (1885), 497 ff.

[3] E. Rohde, 'Die asianische Rhetorik und die zweite Sophistik', *Rh. Mus.* 41 (1886), 170 ff. = *Kl. Schr.* (1901) 2. 75 ff.

[4] E. Norden, *Die antike Kunstprosa* (1915), pp. 351–92, which appeared in the first edition of 1898.

[5] U. von Wilamowitz, 'Asianismus und Attizismus', *Hermes* 35 (1900), 1 ff. Cf. the very sensible remarks on this controversy by A. E. Douglas in *CQ* N.S. 5 (1955), 241–7, and in his commentary on Cicero's *Brutus* (1966), p. xiii.

[6] Cf. U. von Wilamowitz, rebuking A. Boulanger in a review of his *Aelius Aristide*: 'Von der schlechthin unbrauchbaren Erfindung des Philostratos, der zweiten Sophistik, hat er sich nicht losgemacht' (*Litteris* 2 [1925], 126).

[7] *VS*, p. 479.

who are not actually sophists but seem to be, and they are therefore so denominated; such philosophers are said to attain the rank of sophist by virtue of fluency.[1] It is fortunate that Philostratus provides guidance in these matters of professional titles, for in the second century they were sometimes important. Of a genuine rivalry between philosophers and rhetors there can be no doubt (let sophists, for the moment, be subsumed in the general category of rhetors), for philosophy and rhetoric constituted the two principal parts of higher education.[2] Their practitioners competed with each other for the allegiance of the young. Because of the nature of their work rhetors were, of course, more eloquent in denouncing philosophers than were philosophers in denouncing rhetors. Among the most powerful assaults on the philosophers is the latter part of Aelius Aristides' Oration on the Four: philosophers, we are told, do not speak or write λόγοι, adorn festival assemblies, honour the gods, advise cities, comfort the distressed, settle civil discord, or educate the young.[3] This remarkable passage is nothing less than a catalogue of the work of a sophist, for it is in the various points enumerated by Aristides that sophists are superior to philosophers. Aristides' antipathy to philosophers was strong, and his strictures were not altogether just. Philosophers had been known to advise cities, comfort the distressed, settle civil discord, and educate the young.

It was, in fact, possible for the professions of philosopher and rhetor to be conflated and confused. They had many tasks in common, and both were obliged to use the spoken and written word. Accordingly, as Philostratus recognized, eloquent philosophers might be numbered among the sophists. As such, Favorinus of Arelate and Dio of Prusa figure in the *Lives of the Sophists*. The two professions are similarly conjoined on inscriptions, confuting Aristides and lending credibility to Philostratus. For example, the poet T. Flavius Glaucus appears on an honorific text as rhetor and philosopher;[4] on an epigram from Athens a man is declared to be a rhetor in his speaking and

[1] Ibid., p. 484: τῶν φιλοσόφων τοὺς ξὺν εὐροίᾳ ἑρμηνεύοντας.
[2] H. I. Marrou, *Histoire de l'éducation dans l'antiquité* (1960), pp. 288 ff. Cf. also M. D. Brock, *Studies in Fronto and his Age* (1911), ch. 8.
[3] Aristid. 46, p. 404 Dindorf.
[4] *Hesperia*, Suppl. 8 (1949), 246 ff.

a philosopher in his thinking.[1] Another man appears as a sophist and philosopher,[2] and examples could be multiplied. There is a notable text in Alexandria in which Aelius Demetrius the rhetor is honoured by a group of philosophers (presumably those of the Museum).[3] Cassius Dio, a contemporary of Philostratus, wrote of Julia Domna that because of the prefect Plautianus' hostility she began to study philosophy and associate with sophists.[4] Philostratus, therefore, accurately reflects the relations of philosophers and sophists in the intellectual milieu of the second century.

In the elucidation of professional titles the distinction between rhetor and sophist poses a far more difficult problem than that of philosopher and rhetor (or sophist). It is clear from sundry texts that there was some kind of distinction felt between the titles ὁ ῥήτωρ and ὁ σοφιστής. Philostratus, on occasion, deliberately eschewed the word 'sophist' in alluding to certain persons,[5] and Galen once wrote of the sophist Hadrian that in his earlier years he was a rhetor but not yet a sophist.[6] However, often on inscriptions the terms 'rhetor' and 'sophist' coexist without discomfort: Dionysius of Miletus, the celebrated Hadrianic sophist, appears in an Ephesian text, for instance, as ῥήτορα καὶ σοφιστήν.[7] Also in a letter to the Koinon of Asia Antoninus Pius can be seen using the word sophist and rhetor interchangeably.[8]

Scholars have put forward various explanations of the terms 'sophist' and 'rhetor'. For some ancient authors anyhow, it has been claimed, a rhetor was exclusively a forensic speaker and

---

[1] Kaibel, *Epigrammata Graeca*, no. 106 = Peek, *Griechische Versinschriften* 588: ῥήτωρ μὲν εἰπεῖν, φιλόσοφος δ' ἃ χρὴ νοεῖν.

[2] Suid., s.v. Hippias of Elis.

[3] E. Breccia, *Cat. général, musée d'Alexandrie, Iscrizioni greche e latine*, no. 146 (an improved text of *OGIS* 712). See C. P. Jones, *CQ* 17 (1967), 311 ff.

[4] Dio 76. 15. 7: φιλοσοφεῖν . . . ἤρξατο καὶ σοφισταῖς συνημερεύειν. Note also Plut. *Quaest. Conv.* 710 B: βαθυπώγων σοφιστὴς ἀπὸ τῆς Στοᾶς.

[5] Observe *VS*, p. 605, where a group of men are designated ἀθύρματα of the Greeks rather than σοφισταὶ λόγου ἄξιοι. However, one of this group, Soterus, is attested on inscriptions at Ephesus and Delphi, indicating that not everyone was of Philostratus' opinion: *JÖAI* 40 (1953), 15–18, and *Fouilles de Delphes* iii. 4 (1954), no. 265, p. 290 (plate 35, 4). Similarly Phylax, attested at Olympia and Delphi: *REG* 80 (1967), 379 ff.

[6] Galen 14. 627 Kühn: ὁ ῥήτωρ οὔπω σοφιστεύων.

[7] *JÖAI* 40 (1953), 6.   [8] *Dig.* 27. 1. 6. 2. See below, pp. 33–4.

a sophist a professor or school teacher.¹ Strabo's phrase σοφιστεύειν τὰ ῥητορικά can be invoked in support of this view; but
Strabo also uses the verb ῥητορεύειν for the same idea.² Certainly for the second century such an interpretation is quite
unacceptable in view of the fact that Aristides, an undoubted
sophist, rarely taught anyone and was opposed to the idea of
teaching for pay.³

On another interpretation the designation of sophist is
purely honorific and ranks higher than that of rhetor.⁴ Yet
this notion is hard to reconcile with certain epigraphical
evidence or the letter of Pius, or—for that matter—with
Galen's phrase. To say, as Galen does, that a man was not yet
a sophist would have to be likened to calling a man a εὐεργέτης
but not yet a κτίστης. Furthermore, Philostratus admits among
his sophists a man like Varus of Laodicea for whom he has the
lowest possible opinion.⁵ More to the point, it seems, is Dessau's
conjecture that a rhetor practises his art in a less polished and
more dilettantish fashion than a sophist.⁶ Philostratus can be
cited in support of his view: he asserts that earlier generations
called sophists not only those rhetors who were fluent and distinguished but also certain philosophers.⁷ The implication is
that sophists represent a category within the general group of
rhetors, which will have been the broader term. The sense
of sophist can perhaps best be had from the modern notion of
professionalism. The sophist was a virtuoso rhetor with a big
public reputation. So when Galen said of Hadrian the Sophist,
ὁ ῥήτωρ οὔπω σοφιστεύων, he probably meant that Hadrian

---

¹ This was the view of R. Jeuckens, *Plutarch und die Rhetorik* (1907), pp. 47–54
('Der Begriff des σοφιστής'). Cf. C. Brandstätter, 'De notionum πολιτικός et
σοφιστής usu rhetorico', *Leipzig. Stud. z. class. Phil.* 15 (1894), 129–274. The
definition of the late rhetorical theorist, Victorinus, is not relevant here: Vict.
Rhet. Lat. Min. 156. 21 Halm.
² Strabo, p. 614 (σοφιστεύειν τὰ ῥητορικά), p. 650 (ἐρρητόρευε).
³ The word 'sophist' is claimed as a term of abuse in Aristides: E. Mensching,
Mnemosyne 18 (1965), 62, n. 3; C. A. Behr, *Aelius Aristides and the Sacred Tales*
(1968), p. 106, n. 39. But cf. Aristid. 50. 100 Keil, which Behr emends.
⁴ This is the view of K. Gerth in his article 'Zweite Sophistik' (unreliable),
P–W Suppl. 8. 723. Note the comment of W. Spoerri on Gerth's article: 'une
mine inépuisable d'inexactitudes et d'erreurs' (*Rev. de Philol.* 41 [1967],
118, n. 1).
⁵ *VS*, p. 620.   ⁶ *Hermes* 25 (1890), 160, n. 1.
⁷ *VS*, p. 484.

had not yet embarked upon his professional, public career as a performing rhetor.

It appears, then, that rhetors and sophists are the same, except that not all rhetors will have been sophists. In Pius' letter to the Koinon the emperor refers to the two groups, γραμματικοί and ῥήτορες / σοφισταί, by the collective phrase οἱ παιδεύοντες ἑκατέραν παιδείαν.[1] He has only teachers in mind, and for that reason he sees no difference between rhetors and sophists, since both might or might not be teachers. He was occupied with the distinction between teachers and non-teachers, and a distinction between professionals and non-professionals was of no concern to him. It was, however, of concern to Sextus Empiricus, who provides a particularly striking support for the interpretation preferred here: sophists, he declares, have reached the peak of rhetorical skill.[2]

It has been necessary to dilate on these titles because much confusion exists, and these things clearly meant something to the sophists themselves. Pride in petty titles looms large in the second century, for cities—as everyone knows—as well as for individual men.[3]

It has sometimes been claimed in support of the view of 'sophist' as a purely honorific term that the careers of Athenaeus' sophists at dinner were not exclusively rhetorical. The diners included philosophers, grammarians, a doctor, a musician, and (possibly) a famous lawyer.[4] The musician is somewhat surprising as a sophist; the others are not. In so far as rhetoric can be a relevant province of various professional persons, the title of sophist is open to them. The case of philosophers has already been examined. It is obvious that lawyers could have been adjudged sophists through forensic rhetoric of a polished kind; and whether or not Athenaeus really included a lawyer among his diners, there is no reason why he should not have

---

[1] See p. 12, n. 8 above.
[2] Sextus Empiricus, adv. math. 2. 18: οἱ σοφιστεύοντες ἐπ' ἄκρον μὲν τὴν ῥητορικὴν ἐξήσκησαν τεχνολογίαν.
[3] On cities' squabbling for titles like μητρόπολις or πρώτη πόλις see D. Magie, Roman Rule in Asia Minor (1950), i. 635–7, ii. 1496, n. 17.
[4] The Ulpian at dinner may or may not be the lawyer: cf. W. Dittenberger, 'Athenäus und sein Werk', Apophoreton (1903), 1 ff., and W. Kunkel, Herkunft und soziale Stellung der römischen Juristen (1952), pp. 245–54.

done so. A doctor's claim to being a sophist can derive, as will emerge in a subsequent chapter,[1] from an interest in philosophy and fluent exposition of his subject. Presumably a musician could be entitled to sophistic rank in much the same way.

Both in his career and in his ideas Philostratus was a representative specimen of the sophistic movement he chronicled. His information came to him directly, either from his own teachers or from others who had known the great sophists of the second century. He was not attempting scholarly or authoritative biography. He was attracted by anecdotes and fond of quoting from the sophists' works (a feature of the *Lives* which may, on occasion, induce tedium). But he could hardly have been better placed to write about the sophistic movement. This is reporting at first hand.

Like many of his subjects, Philostratus had a career closely bound up with the imperial court and with certain leading Romans. The intimate relation between sophists and the masters of the empire must not, however, deceive. The men of whom Philostratus wrote were Greeks, in the broad sense— from Greece, Asia Minor, Syria, Egypt. Favorinus from Gaul was a special case (in this and in other respects too),[2] but his culture was indubitably Hellenic. These men were not oblivious of their tradition, and when they became so integral a part of the Roman world it was not because they turned upon their inheritance. On the contrary, their preoccupation with the glorious past of their ancient predecessors became more conspicuous. It is everywhere apparent, in their teaching, their examples, the very topics of their discourse. This is not because the sophists were eaten up by nostalgia for the old times, nor were they affirming the independent greatness of the Greeks against the Romans. They bore no grudge for belonging to the Roman empire; they did not object to the word ʿΡωμαῖοι, a collective and non-prejudicial term.[3] In fact, if there was any submergence of one nationality in another, it was at times the Roman which gave way to the Greek. The emperor Hadrian was, after all, a thoroughgoing philhellene; and Marcus

---

[1] See Chapter V below.   [2] He was a hermaphrodite (*VS*, p. 489).

[3] Cf. J. Palm, *Rom, Römertum, und Imperium in der griechischen Literatur der Kaiserzeit* (1959), and G. W. Bowersock, *JRS* 58 (1968), 261 f.

Aurelius wrote his meditations like a Greek and in Greek. But there had been Roman philhellenes for centuries, not however —apart from Nero—conspicuously on the throne of the Caesars. It was possible for a proud Greek to be a Roman without any loss of national pride or abnegation of cultural tradition. Aelius Aristides' panegyric of Rome can *only* be understood when read in conjunction with his other speeches in praise of cities, the panegyrics of Cyzicus, Corinth, Athens, Rhodes, Smyrna.[1] These were all cities of the same world, Rome included in it.[2]

Within that great and hitherto unparalleled οἰκουμένη Greeks and Romans dwelt together, sharing in friendship and government without sacrifice of national integrity. The age had common tastes which worked themselves out in different ways according to different traditions. This proves the point. It is no secret that the second century shows a predilection for antiquity and archaism, and this predilection extended from East to West, dominating the literary activity of Greeks and Romans. But the Greeks looked back to Athens of the fifth century and to Attic purity, whereas the Romans turned to the Punic Wars, studying the old Cato and exploring archaic Latin vocabulary. The mood was shared in common; its expression was appropriately diverse. To see a serious nationalistic split in (at any rate) the cultivated classes of the Roman empire in the second century would be to miss perhaps the most striking feature of the age and something quite unique in ancient history. The equilibrium was far from perfect, and there was doubtless dissatisfaction in lower strata of society; moreover, personal ambition and chaotic rule can make any imperial coherence transitory, and did. But Philostratus and his sophists, with all the attendant witnesses of inscriptions and papyri, are a reliable evocation of a grand baroque age before its dissolution, an age in which Herodes Atticus and Cornelius Fronto could be consuls at Rome in the same year.[3]

[1] D. Nörr, *Imperium und Polis in der hohen Prinzipatszeit* (1966), pp. 83 ff. makes much use of the εἰς 'Ρώμην but is largely ignorant of Aristides' other panegyrics. The attempt of J. Bleicken to extract what is original in the εἰς 'Ρώμην is more substantial: *NGA* 1966, 7, pp. 225–77. Cf. H. Bengtson, *Gymnasium* 71 (1964), 150 ff.
[2] It is worth observing that at Greek games encomia of members of the imperial house were among the fields of competition: cf., e.g., *SEG* 3. 334; *Corinth*, VIII. 3. 153 (on which *REG* 79 [1966], 743).   [3] Namely A.D. 143.

II

CITIES OF THE SOPHISTS

FROM the abundant evidence for the origins of sophists and the cities (other than Rome) in which they taught, it is not difficult to make out which were the great sophistic centres. Above all ranked Athens, Smyrna, and Ephesus. These three cities produced many of the eminent sophists of the second century and received most of the others at some time during their careers. The sophistic revival was an important part of the new prestige and economic vigour which accrued to these cities under the high empire. The sophists and their families were wealthy and could do much through holding magistracies and underwriting the costs of new buildings. And their fame attracted the rich and cultivated (the ones who could afford to travel) from distant regions of the empire. Polemo drew his audiences from both continents and thereby, says Philostratus, caused Smyrna to become more populous.[1] The pupils of Scopelian, it is claimed, had come from Greece, Egypt, Assyria, Phoenicia, and Cappadocia, as well as western Asia Minor.[2] And throngs heard the declamations of Herodes in Agrippa's theatre at Athens.[3]

When one thinks of the unstable economic condition of Athens as the principate began or the modest prosperity which Strabo signals in Ephesus,[4] the vast difference becomes at once striking, wrought in no small measure by cultural distinctions. The visitor to ancient Ephesus today sees the magnificent remains of a substantially second-century city, in which lie

---

[1] *VS*, p. 531.

[2] *VS*, p. 518. Notice also the diverse origins of the pupils of Soterus as recorded on an Ephesian inscription: *JÖAI* 40 (1953), 16.

[3] The Agrippeum was the place for public declamations in imperial Athens. Cf., e.g., *VS*, pp. 571, 579. It was located in the Agora and has been uncovered by the American School of Classical Studies: *Hesperia* 19 (1950), 31 ff.

[4] Cf. J. Day, *An Economic History of Athens under Roman Domination* (1942), pp. 120 ff.; Strabo 641 (Ephesus).

numerous statues, statue-bases, and inscriptions commemorating sophists of the age. Smyrna cannot have been very different, and what has emerged of its agora suggests as much. As for Athens, nearly all its rich past has given up fragments, large and small; and among them are, for example, the library of Pantainos and the Olympieum completed under Hadrian. It will not be forgotten that Polemo delivered an address at the consecration of that temple.[1] The establishment of chairs of rhetoric and philosophy at Athens confirmed an eminence the city had already acquired.[2]

The greatness of Athens, Smyrna, and Ephesus is proved— quite apart from the numbers of sophists associated with those cities and the prosperity they enjoyed—by the simple fact that sophists who were born in them stayed there. They travelled abroad, of course, but their birthplaces remained the centres of their professional activity. So with Herodes Atticus at Athens, Damian at Ephesus, Rufinus at Smyrna. The only native of any of the three cities who can be said with certainty to have transferred his activity elsewhere was the worthy Lollianus of Ephesus, who went to Athens to become the first incumbent of a new chair of rhetoric.[3] It was an academic *Ruf* of distinction and could scarcely be refused.

Sophists born outside the cultural centres moved regularly to one of them. Thus Dionysius went from Miletus to Ephesus, Polemo from Laodicea to Smyrna, Pollux from Naucratis to Athens.[4] Examples are numerous. Many sophists from lesser places were often on tour, settling only temporarily at a sophistic centre. Alexander the Clay-Plato made several visits to Athens, but he is said to have taught at Antioch, Rome, Tarsus, and in Egypt.[5] Even so delicate a creature as Aelius Aristides travelled far from his native Hadrianoutherai in the earlier part of his career; he visited Egypt and passed, in considerable pain, over the Via Egnatia to Rome.[6] To be sure, like many

[1] *VS*, p. 533.   [2] Cf. *VS*, pp. 566–7.
[3] *VS*, p. 526. This was a municipal chair: Theodotus was the first professor on an imperial salary (*VS*, p. 566). On Lollianus, cf. O. Schissel, *Philologus* 82 (1926), 181 ff.
[4] *VS*, pp. 526, 568 (Dionysius), 530–1 (Polemo), 593 (Pollux).
[5] *VS*, p. 572.
[6] *VS*, pp. 581–5, together with Aristides' own extant autobiography in the

others, he finally established himself as a sophist in Smyrna, after having been for some years a patient of Asclepius in Pergamum.[1] The origins and movements of the sophists, when reviewed comprehensively, indicate that there were certain other centres of the sophistic art in the East, although none could be compared with the principal three.[2] Pergamum was the home of several important sophists, who evidently remained there to teach: one of these, Aristocles, was a Roman consul, and his biography was written by Philostratus.[3] It was undoubtedly the medical staff connected with the Pergamene Asclepieum which was responsible for the development of sophistic studies; the relation between sophists and doctors was close, as the word ἰατροσοφιστής testifies.[4] In the reign of Augustus Pergamum was a decaying city, when the god Asclepius summoned one Julius Quadratus from the village of Thermae Theseos to restore its fortunes. This we know from the writings of Aristides, who for reasons of health knew Pergamum well.[5] Quadratus must have been both clever and wealthy; his arrival presaged the renaissance of Pergamum, and his descendants of the second century illustrate it.

The temple of Asclepius at Aegae in Cilicia was probably another breeding ground of sophists. Antiochus the sophist passed many a night in the care of the god there, and we happen to know that Antiochus was born at Aegae.[6] A certain Maximus of Aegae, author of a work on Apollonius of Tyana, was also probably a sophist.[7] Byzantium has some claim as

ἱεροὶ λόγοι. On Egypt, see Aristid. 36 Keil; for the journey to Rome, Aristid. 48. 60 Keil.

[1] Cf. Philostratus' biography and Aristides' autobiography (foregoing note).

[2] It is worth observing that at a dramatic date of c. A.D. 75 Mytilene is listed along with Ephesus as an eastern centre of rhetoric: Tac. *Dial.* 15. 3. The explanation of this allusion is probably the distinguished career of Potamo (*IGR* 4. 33). Cf. C. Cichorius, *Rom und Mytilene* (1888), p. 62.

[3] *VS*, pp. 567–8.   [4] See Chapter V below, especially pp. 66–7.

[5] Aristid. 30. 9 Keil: perhaps in connection with the consecration of the temple to Augustus in Pergamum (Dio 51. 20. 7). On Aristides' authorship of Orat. 30 Keil, cf. Wilamowitz, *Litteris* 2 (1925), 126, firmly rejecting Keil's attribution to an anonymous writer.

[6] *VS*, p. 568. Cf. L. Robert, *La Carie* ii, pp. 318–19 for an inscription mentioning, in all probability, Antiochus of Aegae.

[7] Philostr. *Vit. Apoll.* 1. 3. 5 (cf. 1. 12. 14). He was an *ab epistulis graecis*; his existence ought not to be questioned.

a lesser centre of sophists in view of two famous persons who were born and taught there, Marcus and Chrestus of Byzantium. Marcus was much admired by both Polemo and the emperor Hadrian.[1] Chrestus was a pupil of Herodes Atticus and himself had many fine pupils, seven of whom are named by Philostratus.[2] However, it would appear that in the general regard by Philostratus' day Byzantium and her two great intellectual glories were largely forgotten. At any rate there is a remarkable coincidence in Philostratus' accounts of Marcus and Chrestus: both sophists are said to be neglected by the Greeks and not to receive the honour they deserve.[3] Perhaps for a time after Septimius Severus' siege of Byzantium, the city's distinctions were not mentioned and gradually passed out of mind.

In the second half of the second century, for reasons that are obscure, a number of important sophists emerged from Naucratis. None of them made his career in that city. Apollonius went off to Macedonia, Pollux and Proclus to Athens, Athenaeus the deipnosophist presumably to Rome, and Ptolemy to world travels.[4] These five men from Naucratis are all known to have flourished in or about the time of Commodus. Almost nothing is revealed of Naucratis under the empire, but it is hard to believe that purely by accident can we single out so many distinguished sophists from that place in virtually the same generation.

One wonders why hardly anything is heard of sophists from Alexandria. The Museum was there; and men from elsewhere, such as Dionysius and Polemo, belonged to it.[5] But very few

---

[1] *VS*, pp. 529–30.

[2] *VS*, pp. 590–1. Among his pupils were Hippodromus the sophist (who was a teacher of Philostratus), the mysterious Aquila from Galatia (on whom cf. A. R. Birley, *Britain and Rome: Essays pres. to E. Birley* [1966], pp. 58–60), and the Athenian Sospis (perhaps a descendant of the dadouchos of *IG* ii/iii². 2342, l. 21; cf. *Hesperia* 10 [1941], 261).

[3] *VS*, pp. 527–8: μήπω τυγχάνει τῆς ἑαυτοῦ δόξης (of Marcus the sophist); p. 590 ἀμελοῦντες ἀνδρός (of Chrestus).

[4] *VS*, p. 599 (Apollonius), p. 593 (Pollux), p. 603 (Proclus), p. 596 (Ptolemy). The *Deipnosophistae* of Athenaeus is set at the house of P. Livius Larensis at Rome (cf. *ILS* 2932).

[5] *VS*, p. 524 (on Dionysius' membership) provides an explanation of the Μουσεῖον: an Egyptian dining-table to which are invited τοὺς ἐν πάσῃ τῇ γῇ ἐλλογίμους. *VS*, p. 532 (Polemo's membership, evidently given to him by the emperor Hadrian).

native Alexandrians seem to appear in the records of the Second Sophistic. Nor is there in this period much word of Syrian Antioch. Yet the catalogue of origins of sophists and rhetors is very extensive. A selective list might include, apart from cities already adduced, Byblos, Gadara, Tyre, Emesa, Tarsus, Tyana, Side, Perge, Aphrodisias, Thyatira, Cnidos, Nicomedia, Amastris, Perinthus, Aenos, Larissa.[1] Then there are those men described simply as Arabian, Cappadocian, Galatian.[2] The origins of sophists are to be found all over the Greek East, and in freak cases from the West (Favorinus came from Arelate). This very diffusion, together with the extensive travel involved in a professional career, attests the coherence of the Graeco-Roman world at that time. However obscure or remote his birthplace, an aspiring youth could well dream—as in Lucian's essay[3]—of fame and influence in the great cities of the empire.

But a sophist's family was generally not obscure, at least locally. The career required journeys and public benefactions, not to mention the fees for instruction by great teachers, fees which were possible only for the wealthy; and the wealthy were the local aristocrats. With the aid of Philostratus and certain ample inscriptions, it is possible to be precise about the social background of the sophists. In three instances only can a low or middle-class origin be made out: the father of Secundus of Athens was a carpenter,[4] Quirinus' family at Nicomedia was—we are told—neither distinguished nor

---

[1] Byblos (Aspasius, *PIR²*, A 1261); Gadara (Valerius Apsines, *PIR²*, A 978 with *Hesperia* 10 [1941], 261); Tyre (Hadrian, *PIR²*, H 4); Emesa (Fronto, Suid. s.v.); Tarsus (Hermogenes, *PIR²*, H 149); Tyana (Aurelius Athenaeus, *Forsch. Eph.* iv. 1, n. 14 = *Hellenica* 2 [1946], 93 addendum); Side (Seccius Trophimus, Kaibel *Epig. Graec.* 772a); Perge (Varus, *VS*, pp. 576–7); Aphrodisias (M. Flavius Antonius Lysimachus, *MAMA* 8. 501 [cf. L. Robert, *Ant. Class.* 35 [1966], 395–6, n. 3]); Thyatira (Aurelius Athenaeus, *AE* 1911. 137); Cnidos (Theagenes, *VS*, p. 564); Nicomedia (Quirinus, *VS*, pp. 620–1); Amastris (Diogenes, *VS*, p. 591); Perinthus (Rufus, *VS*, pp. 597–8); Aenos (Athenodorus, *VS*, pp. 594–5); Larissa (Hippodromus, *VS*, pp. 615–20).

[2] Heliodorus of Arabia: *VS*, pp. 625–7; Diodotus of Cappadocia: *VS*, p. 617; Aquila of Galatia: *VS*, p. 591.

[3] Cf. Lucian, *Somnium* 11.

[4] *VS*, p. 544. This sophist ought to be identified with the legendary Hadrianic figure Secundus the Silent Philosopher. B. E. Perry, *Secundus the Silent Philosopher* (1964) denies the identification, but see Appendix I below. On Secundus, see also the inscription associated with him: *Hesperia* 35 (1966), 248–9.

obscure,[1] and Apollonius of Naucratis began his career as a household hireling in Macedonia.[2] There were doubtless others, neglected by Philostratus, who attained some eminence from modest beginnings. There was even a report that the influential Dionysius of Miletus came of unimpressive parentage.[3] But the evidence is overwhelming that sophists almost always emerged from the notable and wealthy families of their cities.

Examples, as often, are numerous, and an illustrative selection should suffice. Aristocles derived from a consular house at Pergamum;[4] Varus of Perge is said explicitly to have been son of one of the most important men in the city.[5] Rufus of Perinthus belonged to a consular house renowned for its great wealth,[6] and the celebrated Damian belonged to a family similarly placed at Ephesus.[7] The parents of Proclus of Naucratis and Heracleides of Lycia were also persons of substance.[8] Something can be said about the family of Philostratus' teacher, Antipater: his father, Zeuxidemus, was one of the most important men in Phrygian Hierapolis.[9] It happens that a P. Aelius Zeuxidemus Cassianus is attested at that Hierapolis as an Asiarch and as father of one P. Aelius Zeuxidemus Aristus Zeno, *advocatus fisci* in the province of Asia.[10] Zeuxidemus Zeno has been identified with the parent of Antipater, as named by Philostratus.[11] One must think of him as at least a close relative of Antipater. Philostratus alludes to a sophist of the early third century by the name of Cassianus;[12] and in view of Zeuxidemus Cassianus, father of Zeuxidemus Zeno, this person should be connected with the house of Antipater at Hierapolis.

Of all the sophists in Philostratus, Polemo and Herodes Atticus take pride of place, both of long-established families

---

[1] *VS*, p. 620. The surprising name Quirinus ought probably to be emended to Quirinius. Observe a Quirinia Patra at Side (*IGR* 3. 810).

[2] *VS*, pp. 599–600.　　　[3] *VS*, p. 521.　　　[4] *VS*, p. 567.

[5] *VS*, p. 576. Note the Varian games at Perge: *JRS* 55 (1965), 54, n. 5; cf. *AE* 1965. 208. There can be scarcely any doubt that Varus the sophist bore the *nomen* Plancius.

[6] *VS*, p. 597.　　　　　　　　　　　　　　　[7] *VS*, p. 605.

[8] *VS*, pp. 602 (Proclus), 612 (Heracleides).　　　[9] *VS*, p. 606.

[10] *IGR* 4. 819; *PIR*², A 281, 282. Cf. H.-G. Pflaum, *Les Carrières procuratoriennes équestres* (1960) i, no. 205, pp. 550–1.　　　[11] Pflaum, ibid.

[12] *VS*, p. 627: his one celebrated pupil was a Lydian.

whose wealth and prestige contributed in no small measure to the Greek renaissance of the second century. The family of Polemo extends back into the late republic: centred in Laodicea on the Lycus, it produced great figures in successive generations—kings in Pontus and Thrace, ambassadors, at least one poet.[1] A relative of the famous sophist reached the consulate in A.D. 148.[2] Polemo's house at Smyrna was the finest in the whole city, and it is well known how he expelled from it Antoninus Pius, who was at that time governing Asia.[3] The sophist retained his ancestral ties with Laodicea, so that both his native city and Smyrna (where he taught) benefited from his patronage.[4]

Like Polemo's, Herodes' ancestors can be traced back to the late republic, and they are found as magistrates, ambassadors, and benefactors.[5] The wealth of Herodes' father was a match for the wealth of his grandfather, whose estate was confiscated ἐπὶ τυραννικαῖς αἰτίαις.[6] Long traditions of education and wealth underlie the Second Sophistic.

Although they are rarely so informative, epigraphical sources support the view of sophists' families as presented by Philostratus. Amphicles of Chalcis, known from the *Lives of the Sophists* to have been a pupil of Herodes, emerges on an inscription as a descendant of consuls.[7] And a less luminous Polemo, namely Ti. Claudius Polemo, appears as an equestrian with a distinguished lineage.[8] A recent text from Athens suggests that Pollux, author of the *Onomasticon* and favourite of Commodus, was a person of considerable wealth.[9] Inscriptions

---

[1] On all this, Bowersock, *Augustus and the Greek World* (1965), pp. 143–4.
[2] M. Antonius Zeno: *PIR²*, A 883.
[3] *VS*, p. 534.   [4] *VS*, p. 532.
[5] Note Herodes of Marathon in the time of Julius Caesar and Eucles in the time of Augustus: *IG* iii². 3175. Cf. P. Graindor, *Un Milliardaire antique: Hérode Atticus et sa famille* (1930), pp. 1–17 ('Les Ancêtres d'Hérode Atticus') and 19–38 ('Atticus', i.e. Herodes' father).
[6] Herodes' father discovered a treasure which more than compensated for the imperial confiscation of his grandfather's estate: *VS*, pp. 547–8. On the grandfather (Hipparchus) and the confiscation see also Suet. *Vesp.* 13, and the important inscription concerning τὰ Ἱππάρχου χωρία τὰ ὑπὸ τοῦ φίσκου πραθέντα, republished accessibly (and with improvements on earlier publications) in J. H. Oliver, *The Ruling Power* (1953), pp. 960–1.   [7] *SIG³* 1240, n. 1.
[8] *PIR²*, C 963. Cf. A. Stein, *Epitymbion H. Swoboda dargebracht* (1927), p. 303.
[9] *Hesperia* 29 (1960), 30 together with 418.

have also revealed the well-connected house of a rhetor called
T. Flavius Menander (senators and consulars in the family);[1]
similarly well placed was the poet, philosopher, and rhetor
T. Flavius Glaucus.[2]

No less conspicuous than the ancestors of sophists in their
cities are their descendants. The Philostrati were not the only
celebrated case of the profession continuing with the same
family, which grew in status in each generation. The house of
Polemo went on to further distinctions after the great sophist:
among other things his granddaughter married the consul
Rufinianus (presumably C. Caesonius Macer Rufinianus),[3]
and they produced a son, by the name of Hermocrates, also
a sophist of note.[4] This Hermocrates was the person to whom
Antipater of Hierapolis betrothed his daughter, with the Emperor's connivance.[5] The marriage did not last; it would have
been a potent nexus, bringing together the élite of Hierapolis
and Laodicea.

The progeny of other sophists merits attention. The pattern
is clear and important. One Apollonius of Athens is discovered from inscriptions as the grandfather of a sophist, P.
Herennius Ptolemaeus. And Ptolemaeus was father to the
historian Dexippus.[6] Again, Nicetes of Smyrna was the ances-
tor of a line of high priests and hoplite generals, and—in
particular—of Euodianus the sophist, whose biography was
written by Philostratus.[7] The son of Flavius Menander the
rhetor had the same name and the same profession.[8]

Especially vexing is the evidence for the house of Julius
Quadratus at Pergamum. Were the details ever to be known
precisely, it is more than likely that the fortunes of this family

[1] *PIR*[2], F 320.

[2] J. H. Oliver, *Hesperia*, Suppl. 8 (1949), 246 ff.

[3] *VS*, p. 609, cf. *ILS* 1182 (C. Caesonius Macer Rufinianus, consul of unknown Severan date).

[4] *VS*, pp. 544, 608–12.   [5] *VS*, pp. 610–11.

[6] *IG* iii[2]. 3665, 3669; *PIR*[2], H 122. The great-grandfather of Dexippus will
not have been the Apollonius of Athens known to us from Philostratus; cf. P.
Graindor, *BCH* 51 (1927), 281. Dexippus' Apollonius was son of a Eudemus; it
would appear that Philostratus' Apollonius was son of an Apollonius (cf.
J. H. Oliver, *Hesperia* 36 [1967], 334–5).

[7] *VS*, p. 596.

[8] *Forsch. Ephesos* 3. 145, no. 62. For more but less conspicuous examples of
the sophistic profession in the same family, see above, p. 4, n. 4.

would be a match for those of Polemo and Herodes Atticus. Not that evidence is lacking: there are several large inscriptions and many literary allusions, and, in addition, the birthday address to Apellas in the corpus of Aelius Aristides.[1] This last provides many items about the descent of the boy Apellas from a certain Quadratus. Although the orator doubtless exaggerates, the connection he describes between the family of Quadratus and the new prosperity of Pergamum obviously has something in it. Both Quadrati who were consuls in 105 were evidently Pergamene: C. Antius A. Iulius Quadratus, *consul ordinarius* and C. Iulius Quadratus Bassus, *consul suffectus*.[2] The latter, though not identical with the Bithynian governor of Pliny's letters, is conceivably related to him; and both consuls should have some connection with the rhetor Julius Bassus known to the elder Seneca.[3] In the second century there appears in Lucian an effeminate sophist named Bassus,[4] while the Palatine Anthology preserves a poem by one Bassus of Smyrna (who need not have been born there).[5] Galen, who came from Pergamum, dedicated a treatise on books to a Bassus.[6] Finally, both Aristides and Philostratus mention a rhetor of the mid second century with the name Quadratus.[7] The evidence is thus abundant and tantalizing, clearly displaying many features of the age: sophists and rhetors placed somehow in a consular family, and one of the children a pupil of a great personality who was (there is no decent reason to deny it) Aristides. The rhetor Quadratus was, Aristides says himself, a companion of his.[8] More than that, he was proconsul of Asia.[9]

[1] Aristid. 30 Keil.
[2] *PIR²*, I 507 (*consul ordinarius*), 508 (*consul suffectus*).
[3] Pliny, *Ep.* 4. 9 (cf. *PIR²*, I 205). Cf. A. N. Sherwin-White, *The Letters of Pliny: A Social and Historical Commentary* (1966), pp. 274 ff. The rhetor Julius Bassus: *PIR²*, I 204. [4] Lucian, *adv. indoctum* 23.
[5] *Anth. Pal.* xi. 72. This Bassus must be distinguished from the Augustan Lollius Bassus, whose poems also appear in the *Anthology*. Cf. C. Cichorius, *Römische Studien* (1922), pp. 308–9, identifying without good reason the Bassus of xi. 72 with Lollius Bassus.
[6] Galen 19. 8 Kühn = 91 Mueller (*De libris propriis*).
[7] Aristid. 50. 63 Keil; *VS*, p. 576. [8] Aristid. 50. 71 Keil.
[9] Ibid. The vexed problem of his identity (which touches upon the date of the martyrdom of Polycarp) is acutely analysed by T. D. Barnes in *JTS* 18 (1967), 434 ff.

In his own city and province a sophist was expected to provide services and benefactions beyond the sheer prestige of his presence, and most obliged. With his money, his intellect, and his influence a sophist was in a particularly favourable position to aid his city, whether it were his native city, his adoptive, or both. It is recorded that Polemo was able to end outbreaks of serious factional strife in Smyrna and that he also helped to administer the affairs of his native Laodicea.[1] The Lycian Heracleides served as high priest in the Koinon of Lycia, but he is also known as an eponymous στεφανηφόρος of Smyrna.[2] The hoplite generalship in Athens was held by several eminent intellectuals, of which the most famous was undoubtedly the philosopher and teacher of Plutarch, Ammonius—hoplite general three times.[3] The Ephesian Lollianus, as hoplite general, was confronted with a bread riot;[4] and it is known that Apollonius of Athens also served in the same office.[5]

The troubles of Aelius Aristides demonstrate that sophists were expected cheerfully to undertake financial and administrative burdens on behalf of city and province. Aristides' stout refusals to serve as high priest of Asia, as a local tax collector in Smyrna, or as an irenarch in Hadrianoutherai were evidently unexpected and anomalous, despite the fact that there existed machinery for the granting of immunities.[6] Most sophists were prepared to suffer the expense and inconvenience of public office in order to enjoy the gratitude of citizens and still higher status. Among sophists known from the second century there are Asiarchs and high priests; without disputing here the controversial relationship of these two offices (which ought to be identical), we may mention as Asiarchs the Flavii Menandri, father and son, Athenaeus of Thyatira, and the equestrian Ti. Claudius Polemo.[7] Attested as high priests are the posterity

---

[1] *VS*, pp. 531–2.   [2] *VS*, pp. 612 (high priest), 613 (στεφανηφόρος).
[3] See now C. P. Jones, 'The Teacher of Plutarch', *HSCP* 71 (1966), 205–13. On hoplite generals there is the register by Th. Sarikakis, *The Hoplite Generals of Athens* (1951), unfortunately not very reliable. It has been supplemented by the studies of D. J. Geagan in *Hesperia*, Suppl. 12 (1967); *The Athenian Constitution after Sulla*, ch. 2.
[4] *VS*, p. 526.   [5] *VS*, p. 600.
[6] On all this see Chap. III below.
[7] For the Flavii Menandri, see p. 24, note 8 above; and for the Polemo, see p. 23, note 8. Athenaeus of Thyatira: *AE* 1911. 137. On the identity of Asiarchs

of Nicetes and Scopelian, also Polemo's great-grandson Hermocrates, and the remarkable Aur. Septimius Apollonius, father
of senators.[1]

Whether holding office or not, sophists were expected to give
freely from their vast funds for the adornment and comfort of
their cities. The benefactions of sophists are a palpable expression of the union of literary, political, and economic influence,
so characteristic of the Second Sophistic. One of the early
representatives of the movement, Nicetes, caused the construction of a splendid approach to Smyrna, so as to connect
with the gate toward Ephesus.[2] Philostratus records that despite the reluctance of Antiochus of Aegae to hold public office
he freely contributed from his own resources to building projects as well as to the food supply.[3] And Heracleides of Lycia
was responsible for a fountain at Smyrna in the gymnasium of
Asclepius.[4] The house of Herodes at Athens provided in staggering abundance for the Athenians: the sophist's father had
bequeathed a mina annually to every Athenian citizen (not
that Herodes carried out his wishes).[5] Herodes himself was
responsible for the great Panathenaic stadium and for a theatre
at Athens with a roof made of cedar.[6] Nor were his enormous
benefactions confined to Athens. One thinks of the theatre at
Corinth, the stadium at Delphi, the baths at Thermopylae,
the aqueduct at Olympia.[7] No sophist could match the lavish
expenditures of Herodes.

Yet the great Damian of Ephesus was able to spend on
a large scale. He is said to have maintained the Ephesian poor
and to have contributed funds to restore any public building
in need of repair.[8] More than that, in order to protect the

and high priests, see the powerful arguments of J. Deininger, *Die Provinzial-
landtage der römischen Kaiserzeit* (1965), pp. 41–50.

[1] *AE* 1960. 80.   [2] *VS*, p. 511.   [3] *VS*, p. 568.
[4] *VS*, p. 613.
[5] *VS*, p. 549. The Athenians agreed to accept a single payment of five minae
each instead of an annual mina, but by a ruse Herodes contrived that no man
should receive even his five minae.
[6] *VS*, pp. 550 (the stadium), 551 (the theatre).
[7] On these and other buildings of Herodes, with remarks about archaeologi-
cal evidence for them, see P. Graindor, *Un Milliardaire antique: Hérode Atticus et
sa famille* (1930), pp. 179–230 ('Hérode le bâtisseur').
[8] *VS*, p. 605.

worshippers of Artemis from rain, he built an elaborate marble
portico to link the city with the Artemisium by way of the gate
toward Magnesia on the Maeander; and he constructed a huge
dining hall made of Phrygian marble in the sanctuary itself.[1]
This refectory is now unfortunately sunk in the wet plain that
lies where the Artemisium used to be, but remains of the great
portico emerged in the early work at Ephesus by J. T. Wood.[2]
    Philostratus reveals that Damian dedicated the portico to his
wife,[3] and we happen to know that she was one of the great
ladies of Ephesus. Her father was P. Vedius Antoninus, son
of an Asiarch and himself a man of public spirit and a certain
affluence.[4] The modern visitor to Ephesus is even now struck
by the initiative of Vedius in the gymnasium he built near the
stadium and in the odeon which lies to the south-east of the
Panayır Dağ. To the east of the odeon were found, in the large
so-called East Gymnasium, statues of Damian and Vedia, his
wife; and the couple, it has been conjectured, presented that
splendid gymnasium to the city of Ephesus.[5] If all the Ephesian
buildings given by the family from which Damian took his
wife be considered in conjunction with his own benefactions,
the agglomeration is almost worthy of a Herodes Atticus. And
it is apposite to observe that among the children of Damian
and Vedia three consuls can be identified and two brides of
consuls.[6]
    The social eminence of the sophists in their cities and pro-
vinces brought their families swiftly and inevitably into the
Roman upper class. In one sense, Rome itself could be numbered among the cities of the sophists; many visited it and

---

    [1] VS, p. 605.
    [2] J. T. Wood, Discoveries at Ephesus (1877), pp. 249–50. J. Keil, JÖAI 40
(1953), 18–20; also W. Alzinger, Die Stadt des siebenten Weltwunders (1962), p. 32.
    [3] VS, p. 605.
    [4] JÖAI 44 (1959), Beibl. 257–9. It appears from SIG³ 850 that Vedius' per-
sonal wealth was not wholly sufficient to finance the grand projects he envisaged for Ephesus: he appealed to the emperor for a subsidy and received one.
    [5] The gymnasium by the stadium: JÖAI 24 (1929), Beibl. 29 ff.; 25 (1929,
sic), Beibl. 21 ff. Odeon: JÖAI 15 (1912), Beibl. 170 ff. East gymnasium: JÖAI
27 (1931), Beibl. 25 ff.; 28 (1933), Beibl. 6 ff.
    [6] See the stemma in PIR², Pars III, p. 178, and the discussion in JÖAI 44
(1959), Beibl., cols. 257–9. The three consuls are T. Flavius Vedius Antoninus
(PIR², F 392), Flavius Damianus (PIR², F 252), and Flavius Phaedrus (PIR²,
F 329), all consuls of unknown Severan date.

some stayed there (especially, of course, after the establishment of a chair of Greek). Rome was a centre for sophists (as
for most things), and it is an old story how the eminent men of
provincial cities left descendants more occupied with careers
in the Roman government than with magistracies and benefactions in their native cities. It was all part of the gradual
transformation of the Roman aristocracy and the concomitant
impoverishment of the curial class in provinces.[1] But in the
second century, when things were still in ferment, gain accrued
both to Rome and to the provincial cities. Herodes Atticus did
not neglect his native Greece because he advanced to the
consulate at Rome. For a time in that century senatorial and
provincial dignity could coincide; and as the houses of sophists
enriched the Roman senate, they also enriched the governing
bodies of their own cities, native or adoptive. But—such is the
nature of historical change—the coherence of the second-
century οἰκουμένη, which allowed the sophists to flourish, also
allowed subsequent generations to pay more attention to Rome
than to the cities from which they came.

[1] For this well-known development see A. H. M. Jones, *The Greek City*
(1940), pp. 189–91, and his 'The Greeks under Roman Rule', *Dumbarton Oaks
Papers* 17 (1963), 3 ff. Cf. also Bowersock, *Augustus and the Greek World* (1965),
pp. 148–9.

III

SPECIAL PRIVILEGES

THE wealth and social standing of the majority of sophists in the second and early third centuries are beyond dispute. Their contributions to the economic revival of cities like Smyrna and Ephesus are patent, and it appears that on the whole the sophists were glad in that age to undertake local magistracies and the attendant financial burdens. Their own prestige and influence were thereby enhanced. Official recognition of the eminence of these men and their families was to be expected from the Roman government: they clearly qualified for special favour. And they received favour, notably in the form of advancement into the equestrian and senatorial orders; the consulate was within reach. In their own cities and provinces the old mode of indicating the government's favour and support, namely bestowal of the Roman citizenship, was becoming increasingly inadequate; most of the sophists had the citizenship already, and in any case too many other people had it for it to be distinctive.[1] But the granting of immunity (ἀτέλεια) still meant something.

Caesar and Augustus had long ago taken care to establish that bestowal of the citizenship should not be thought to entail immunity from taxation or liturgy.[2] Some new Roman citizens in those days had evidently been claiming exemptions. If such

---

[1] On the spread of the Roman citizenship, cf. C. B. Welles, *Bulletin of the American Society of Papyrologists* 2 (1965), 75–7. Of course, compared with the total number of persons in the Roman empire, those possessing the citizenship were few (A. H. M. Jones, *Dumbarton Oaks Papers* 17 [1963], 6), but within the upper-class milieu of the provinces it was ceasing to be a very noticeable distinction.

[2] Cf. Bowersock, *Augustus and the Greek World* (1965), p. 89. The Augustan evidence is the Third Cyrene Edict, which has recently been reinterpreted in a new way by K. M. T. Atkinson, *Ancient Society and Institutions: Studies pres. to V. Ehrenberg* (1966), pp. 21–36. Among other things she assumes that ἀνεισφορία in that document alludes to exemption not from financial obligations to Cyrene but from the payment of tribute to Rome (p. 31).

claims had been generally recognized, financial disaster could have ensued for many provincial cities. Obviously the men and families most likely to receive the citizenship were also those wealthy persons most needed by the cities; if they were not to perform local liturgies, they had at least to provide voluntary benefactions or else the cities would suffer. It is difficult to determine just how great the immediate danger was in the second half of the first century B.C., but the wise precaution of Caesar and Augustus—induced by the lack of public spirit of some provincial citizens—safeguarded the economies of the cities. Immunities in various degrees were therefore infinitely less common throughout the empire than the citizenship and could accordingly constitute a meaningful recognition of a man's attainments in his own province.

However, the importance of an immunity in any given instance depended upon the wealth of the recipient and the closeness of his connection with a provincial city. When Augustus granted ἀτέλεια to doctors as a token of gratitude to the freedman, M. Antonius Musa,[1] no city was going to feel the pinch. But if many of the great second-century sophists were to receive and to claim immunities, it could mean substantial troubles for the eastern cities. Although the evidence is clear for the willingness of most sophists to undertake financial and administrative burdens (as well as to spend lavishly on their own initiative), there exists no less clear evidence that in some way they were entitled to honorific immunities and that in some instances these immunities were claimed. Nor was everyone who claimed them always so generous as Antiochus of Aegae in refusing to hold office but spending money nevertheless in the public interest.[2] There was a ruinous incompatibility between the honour of immunity and economic prosperity in provincial cities—unless those who received immunity did not wish to claim it (so that they could be said to hold office or to spend voluntarily) or unless the very wealthy could be kept from receiving immunities at all (even though they might think themselves entitled to them). The positive contributions of sophists stand on record. The evidence for their

---

[1] Dio 53. 30. 3. Cf. Suet. *Aug.* 59; 81. 1. Doctors in the Augustan age were not men of the upper class, as the sophists were. [2] *VS*, p. 568.

immunity, legal, literary, and epigraphical, has now to be
reviewed and assessed.

First, texts from the *Digest*. The testimony of Charisius is
often adduced: 'Magistris, qui civilium munerum vacationem
habent, item grammaticis et rhetoribus et medicis et philo-
sophis, ne hospitem reciperent, a principibus fuisse immuni-
tatem indultam et divus Vespasianus et divus Hadrianus
rescripserunt.'[1] This statement is inexact.[2] Other evidence,
which will emerge, indicates edicts rather than rescripts, and
the conjunction of Vespasian and Hadrian in respect of a category of teachers that includes philosophers is clearly wrong.
This can be said confidently because of the existence of an
important inscription from Pergamum recording an edict of
Vespasian on the subject of immunity for teachers, who are
specified as doctors and teachers.[3] Vespasian's edict must
underlie Charisius' reference to that emperor. It appears that
Vespasian was the first to grant an immunity to a whole class
of teachers,[4] although limited acts of favour had occurred
before his reign. Such was Julius Caesar's bestowal of the
citizenship on teachers of the liberal arts at Rome.[5] (Augustus
granted exemption from taxation to *medici*.[6]) It is clear from
the Pergamene inscription that there was no provision for
philosophers among the exempted *praeceptores*, nor would we
expect anything of that sort from an emperor who expelled
philosophers from Rome.[7] The reference to Hadrian in Charisius' remark is there because he was apparently the emperor
who incorporated philosophers as a class in the group of
privileged teachers, and that might well have been expected
from such a man.[8]

---

[1] *Dig.* 50. 4. 18. 30.
[2] Cf. R. Herzog, 'Urkunden zur Hochschulpolitik der römischen Kaiser',
Sitzungsberichte preuss. Akad. 1935, p. 983: 'Diese Angabe erweist sich jedoch als
sehr ungenau.' Herzog prints the Charisius text with Cuiacius' *id est* instead of
the transmitted *item* (which stands in Mommsen's edition). With either reading,
Charisius' statement is 'sehr ungenau'.
[3] The inscription was published and discussed by Herzog, op. cit., pp. 967–
1019. It is reproduced in McCrum and Woodhead, *Documents of the Flavian
Emperors* (1961), no. 458.
[4] Cf. Herzog, op. cit., p. 984.   [5] Suet. *Jul.* 42.
[6] See p. 31, note 1 above.
[7] Vespasian's expulsion of philosophers: Dio 65. 13. 2; Suet. *Vesp.* 13, 15.
[8] Herzog, op. cit., pp. 983 f.; D. Magie, *Roman Rule in Asia Minor* (1950), ii.

The case of Flavius Archippus in the tenth book of Pliny's *Letters* indicates that there was no general immunity for philosophers at that time.[1] Archippus had received the special favour of Domitian, and Nerva had confirmed it. Again under Trajan Archippus requested relief, *ut philosophus*, from service on a jury, and Pliny was obliged to provide Trajan with a dossier to prove the previous personal privileges extended to Archippus. With Hadrian the privilege of μὴ κρίνειν (with others) was made available to philosophers as a whole as well as to ῥήτορες, γραμματικοί, and ἰατροί.[2] The evidence is from Modestinus, quoting an edict of Commodus which includes a paragraph from an edict of Pius. And the passage from Pius' edict cites an edict of Hadrian in which philosophers, rhetors, grammatici, and doctors are declared immune from various liturgies, priesthoods, and billeting; they are also not obliged to serve against their will as judges, ambassadors, or soldiers, nor are they to be forced to undertake any other civic duty. These broad and generous provisions could have been crippling for many cities, if large numbers of the privileged persons claimed their exemptions. The edict seems a characteristic specimen of Hadrianic cultural enthusiasm, but it also suggests that widespread refusals from cultivated local aristocrats were not anticipated.[3] The edict would simply permit local worthies to acquire the additional merit of performing costly or burdensome services when they were not required to.

But the legal texts from Modestinus reveal that Hadrian's extravagance in the matter of immunities could not be tolerated. Pius imposed strict limits: small cities were allowed five immune doctors, three sophists (or rhetors), and three grammatici; moderate-sized cities could have seven immune doctors, four rhetors, and four grammatici; and the biggest cities could

---

1431. Cf. R. Syme, 'Hadrian as an Intellectual', *Les Empereurs romains d'Espagne* (1965), 243–9.

[1] Pliny, *Ep.* 10. 58. Sherwin-White, *The Letters of Pliny: A Social and Historical Commentary* (1966), pp. 640–1, implies (despite reference to Herzog's publication [p. 32, n. 2 above]) that philosophers in general received special privileges from the Flavian emperors.

[2] *Dig.* 27. 1. 6. 8.

[3] On early indications of refusal to assume local burdens, see *Phoenix* 18 (1964), 327–8. On voluntary benefactions, which were expected or almost obligatory, cf. D. Magie, *Roman Rule in Asia Minor* (1950), i. 654.

have ten immune doctors, five rhetors, and an equal number of grammatici. No city, however large, was allowed more than these. As for philosophers, Pius made it virtually impossible for them to be immune at all. In one of his wittiest pronouncements he declared that a strict limit on the number of exempt philosophers was not set. 'I feel sure', the Emperor remarked, 'that those who are wealthy will voluntarily provide financial assistance to their cities. And if they quibble about the size of their estate, they will thereby make it quite clear that they are not really philosophers.'[1] In other words, philosophers whose wealth could be of any use were effectively removed from the class of the exempt. These firm measures of Pius must mean that the vague generality of Hadrian's edict had proved more dangerous than had been anticipated or else that Pius thought it might be dangerous. There must have been some reason to suspect that too many persons, whose services could not easily be dispensed with, might actually claim the exemptions to which they were entitled under Hadrian's edict. This, of course, has some bearing on the question of the earliest indications of reluctance to hold local office in the East.[2]

The immunity provisions of Pius included one further clause. Members of the four relevant groups might be released from liturgies above the allowed number of ἀτελεῖς if they were not practising in their native territory and if they were ἄγαν ἐπιστήμονες. The latter condition is reminiscent of the provisions for philosophers in its discouragement of exceptional awards of immunity. It must be observed that under the terms of Pius' edict the designation of the permitted ἀτελεῖς in a city was to be made by the local βουλή in each case. It is hard to imagine that such a body would ever decide to include in its list men of outstanding wealth. In short, the arrangements of Hadrian were evidently seen to be a mistake, for Pius' substantial modifications made it very difficult for a man who mattered to a city's economy to secure immunity.

Next, the attested cases of reluctance. They are, it has to be emphasized, few in comparison with the many known magistracies and benefactions of sophists. But it is a fact that

[1] Dig. 27. 1. 6. 7: φανεροὶ γενήσονται μὴ φιλοσοφοῦντες.
[2] See p. 33, n. 3 above.

people nevertheless existed in the second century or early third who were unwilling to serve and to spend, and their cases complement the account already given of the measures of Pius.

The first exhibit is Favorinus of Arelate. Philostratus reports that he was appointed high priest ἐς τὰ οἴκοι πάτρια,[1] an expression normally taken to indicate Arelate, but the high priesthood ought rather to be the flaminate of the Narbonensian *concilium*. Favorinus wished to excuse himself from this burden in accordance with existing laws on the ground that he was a philosopher. He presented his request to the emperor, unnamed in Philostratus but certainly Hadrian. Favorinus perceived that the emperor was unsympathetic to him ὡς μὴ φιλοσοφοῦντι and thereupon found it discreet to abandon his claim, for the reason that his teacher, Dio of Prusa, had appeared to him in a dream and advised him to undertake the liturgy.[2] The claim of Favorinus will have been made under the general edict of Hadrian, which—it has been seen—was the first to include philosophers. It is relevant to stress that Favorinus sought his immunity from the emperor himself, whether at first or only after earlier denials by lesser officials. Cassius Dio, in his account of Favorinus' petition, asserts that Hadrian disliked Favorinus,[3] but this may only be an inference from the affair itself. Hadrian's declared reason for not favouring him was that he was not in fact a philosopher, and this parallels precisely the language of Pius in his explanation of the absence of philosophers from the new immunity regulations. One is left to wonder whether Hadrian himself had not already begun to find his edict impractical,[4] and whether Hadrian's response to Favorinus (and perhaps other philosophers) did not provide Pius with the idea and language of his pronouncement.

Earlier in his biography of Favorinus, Philostratus reports a dispute with the emperor Hadrian,[5] and a suspicion arises that the immunity affair is meant. However, it need not be.

---

[1] *VS*, p. 490.   [2] Ibid.   [3] Dio 69. 3. 4–6.
[4] The edict belongs to the beginning of Hadrian's reign: παρελθὼν εὐθὺς ἐπὶ τὴν ἀρχήν (*Dig.* 27. 1. 6. 8).
[5] *VS*, p. 489: a διαφορά.

Certainly that dispute is what Favorinus himself used to refer to in enumerating the three paradoxes of his life : he was a Gaul who spoke Greek, a eunuch who was prosecuted on an adultery charge, and a man who quarrelled with an emperor and lived.[1] Philostratus says himself that despite Favorinus' trouble with Hadrian, οὐδὲν ἔπαθεν.[2] The evidence implies, whether immunity was at issue or not, that Favorinus did not suffer at the hands of Hadrian.

Yet most modern accounts assert that the philosopher-sophist was exiled by Hadrian. This is an inference from Favorinus' own disquisition on exile, which has survived on papyrus.[3] As a stylized literary production taking its place among numerous treatises on exile, Favorinus' essay has considerable interest and importance. As witness to a hitherto unknown and by no means slight historical fact, it deserves close scrutiny. At one point the text does indeed suggest that Favorinus was writing from exile on Chios,[4] and, if that is right, it becomes necessary to give special weight to the verb 'live' in Favorinus' paradox: he quarrelled with an emperor and *lived*, that is to say—he survived. A similar construction may perhaps be put on οὐδὲν ἔπαθεν, but less easily. The problem stands unresolved; the exile is by no means secure fact. If the dispute with Hadrian did lead to exile, it must not be conflated with the immunity plea, which Favorinus abandoned.

The next exhibit among the immunity cases is the eloquent hypochondriac Aelius Aristides. Thanks to his prolixity, we know more about his case than anyone else's. The long and excruciating story is told in the second half of the Fourth Sacred Discourse; it is not always easy to follow because it is told in reverse (or rather upwards, as Aristides would say). Aristides first mentions his negotiations with the mysterious

---

[1] *VS*, p. 489: Γαλάτης ὢν ἑλληνίζειν, εὐνοῦχος ὢν μοιχείας κρίνεσθαι, βασιλεῖ διαφέρεσθαι καὶ ζῆν.   [2] Ibid.
[3] Φαβωρίνου περὶ φυγῆς, published by M. Norsa and G. Vitelli in *Studi e Testi* 53 (1931), conveniently republished in A. Barigazzi, *Opere: Favorino di Arelate* (1966), pp. 375–409. The inference about Favorinus' exile appears in Norsa–Vitelli, op. cit., p. x; E. Mensching, *Favorin von Arelate* (1963), p. 2; A. Barigazzi, op. cit., pp. 6 and 465; *PIR²*, F 123.
[4] Περὶ φυγῆς (cf. foregoing note) col. 14: Θησεὺς δ' ἂν ὀκνῆσαί σοι δοκεῖ ἐπὶ Χίου ἐκ Μίμαντος μικρὰν θάλασσαν περαιώσασθαι;

governor (and his friend) Quadratus,[1] then his protracted dealings with Quadratus' predecessor Severus (C. Julius Severus, consul *c.* 138, one supposes),[2] next his appeal to Severus' predecessor Pollio (a Vitrasius Pollio, consul *c.* 137),[3] and after that his appeal to a Glabrio some time before Pollio.[4] (The Glabrio appears not to have been a proconsul of Asia at all—the only one not a governor in Aristides' series—if at any rate he is identical with the Acilius Glabrio attested as proconsul's legate in Asia.[5]) To restore the immunity appeals of Aristides to their natural chronological order: he dealt successively with Glabrio, Pollio, Severus, and Quadratus.

Under Glabrio the people of Smyrna proposed Aristides for the high priesthood of Asia, a post laden with honour, time-consuming, and expensive.[6] Aristides' illness seemed neither now nor later to deter persons from proposing him for liturgies. Assisted by encouraging dreams, Aristides persuaded the people to alter their plan, but instead—cleverly—they nominated him to serve as priest of Asclepius: a new temple was then under construction, and Aristides, whose health was in the care of Asclepius, could pay for it. But, of course, the sophist could not undertake any such thing without the bidding of the god himself. In the end the Smyrnaeans put forward Aristides' name at a meeting of the Koinon, and he was obliged to appeal

---

[1] Aristid. 50. 63 ff. Keil. On the identity of Quadratus, see T. D. Barnes, *JTS* 18 (1967), 434 ff.; and below, pp. 84–5.

[2] Aristid. 50. 71 ff. Keil. On the identity of Severus, R. Syme, *JRS* 43 (1953), 159 and *REA* 61 (1959), 311. Also W. Hüttl, *Antoninus Pius* ii (1933), pp. 51–2; C. A. Behr, *Aelius Aristides and the Sacred Tales* (1968), p. 80.

[3] Aristid. 50. 94 ff. Keil. This is not Vitrasius Pollio, consul II in 176: R. Syme, *JRS* 43 (1953), 159 and *REA* ᶠ 1 (1959), 311.

[4] Aristid. 50. 97 ff. Keil. In section 100 he is called, it seems, ὁ σοφιστής. Behr considers σοφιστής a corruption: op. cit., pp. 65–6, n. 17.

[5] Cf. *PIR*², A 73 (*cos. ord.* 152): Groag identified the man in Aristides with the Acilius Glabrio of *ILS* 1072, a difficult cursus to interpret (cf. R. Syme, *REA* 67 [1965], 345–6). For the conviction that Glabrio was a proconsul; W. Hüttl, op. cit. ii (1933), p. 49 (altered to Groag's opinion in i [1936], p. 361). C. A. Behr, op. cit., pp. 65–7, thinks that Glabrio was legate to a proconsul whom he identifies as the honorand of *CIL* 2. 6084.

[6] Aristid. 50. 101 Keil. Avoiding the technical phrase, Aristides says τὴν ἱερωσύνην τὴν κοινὴν τῆς Ἀσίας. The story of Aristides' immunity troubles was briefly surveyed by A. Boulanger, *Aelius Aristide* (1923), pp. 138 ff. and C. A. De Leeuw, *Aelius Aristides* (1939), pp. 16 ff. Cf. now also C. A. Behr, op. cit., pp. 63 ff.

directly to the governor.[1] Satisfaction ensued, but not for long. The governor's ruling was evidently only *ad hoc*. When Pollio was in Asia, the Smyrnaeans again endeavoured to exploit Aristides in what can only have been the way sophists were usually exploited. What one notices is the persistence in the face of an immunity secured not long before. Aristides was chosen ἐκλογεύς of Smyrna, presumably to deal with arrears of taxes, and the choice was confirmed by a proconsul's legate (an interesting indication of the role of Roman provincial officials in local government).[2] Aristides says that he was granted the right of appeal to Rome.[3] Meanwhile, he had letters dispatched at once to the governor and to his legate.[4] Pollio was most obliging and saw to it that the legate altered his previous confirmation.[5] So Aristides was again safe.

After the arrival of Severus as governor the most difficult of the immunity troubles arose, for Aristides' native village of Hadrianoutherai had put forward the sophist's name, among others, for the governor's consideration in the appointment of irenarch—another serviceable item about Roman control of provincial offices.[6] Severus was a man of scrupulous rectitude, as Aristides gladly admits.[7] Such a man was at first unwilling to disqualify a person so wealthy and important as Aristides from a provincial liturgy. Aristides had to produce evidence of powerful support from Rome: letters on his behalf came from Antoninus Pius himself and from Marcus Aurelius. Another came from Aristides' friend, Avidius Heliodorus, former prefect of Egypt.[8] Moved by these documents, Severus openly acknowledged Aristides' preeminence in rhetoric. He confirmed the ἀτέλεια but requested Aristides to serve as irenarch anyhow.[9] It appears from this that he thought Aristides was

[1] Aristid. 50. 102 Keil (the temple of Asclepius), 50. 103 (the Koinon).
[2] Aristid. 50. 96 Keil. This item was not noticed by D. Nörr, *Imperium und Polis in der hohen Prinzipatszeit* (1966).
[3] Aristid. 50. 91 Keil.   [4] Ibid.
[5] Aristid. 50. 98 Keil.
[6] Aristid. 50. 72 Keil: φύλακα τῆς εἰρήνης, again not the technical term. Also not noticed by Nörr (n. 2 above).
[7] Aristid. 50. 71 Keil: ἀνὴρ ὑψηλὸς τοὺς τρόπους καὶ ὅτι γνοίη καὶ προσέλοιτο οὐκ ἂν ὑφεῖτο οὐδενί.
[8] Aristid. 50. 75 Keil. On C. Avidius Heliodorus, see *PIR*², A 1405.
[9] Aristid. 50. 87 Keil.

objecting to a compulsory liturgy, so that Severus' request shows a consistent point of view with the removal of compulsion under the terms of Hadrian's edict. However, the necessity for Aristides to claim immunities—and repeatedly—proves clearly that the new arrangements of Pius were in force. Equally clear is the fact that Aristides had not been enrolled among the permitted number of immune sophists. He will have had to make his claim under the clause providing for those who taught outside their own cities and were ἄγαν ἐπιστήμονες.

Not surprisingly, Aristides found Severus' confirmation of the ἀτέλεια unsatisfactory. The request rather than compulsion did not suit him, because he honestly did not want to serve at all. And the precedent set by Severus would have generated similar immunity crises under each new proconsul. As it was, the decisions of Glabrio and Pollio had only temporary effect and were obviously no deterrent to the people of Asia in subsequent nominations. Feeling that it was necessary to secure a definite and durable immunity, Aristides persisted in his negotiations with Severus after taking the advice and securing the intercession of several of his influential Asian friends, such as the Pergamene L. Cuspius Pactumeius Rufinus (consul in 142) who happened to be at Pergamum at that very time.[1] Severus, scrupulous as ever, was slow to be persuaded, observing, 'There is no dispute about Aristides' eloquence. But it is one thing to be first of the Greeks in eloquence and another to teach and have pupils.'[2] The immunity legislation for rhetors and sophists was in all its developments concerned with teachers, as can easily be seen from Vespasian's word παιδευταί, or from Pius' expression οἱ παιδεύοντες ἑκατέραν παιδείαν.[3] Most great sophists did have pupils, or rather disciples, who spread the fame of the master; Aristides, however, was not a teacher, even though he may have had a few pupils. The objection raised by Severus was not one that can have made much difference generally in the immunity status of

[1] Aristid. 50. 83 Keil. On Rufinus, see *PIR*², C 1637 and below, p. 86.
[2] Aristid. 50. 87 Keil.
[3] For Vespasian's edict, see Herzog (p. 32, n. 2 above); for Pius' edict, see *Dig.* 27. 1. 6. 2, and p. 34 above.

rhetors and sophists. In this point Aristides' case was anomalous, but Severus' statement does serve to illustrate and support the legal texts we possess.

At this juncture in Aristides' affairs the Smyrnaeans, undaunted by his efforts and desire, elected him *prytanis*.[1] Thus two claims for immunity came simultaneously before Severus. The climax of Aristides' long struggle was an interminable oration before the governor in which the orator spoke freely of himself and his association with emperors.[2] Severus was overcome; and he granted Aristides the long-sought immunity, which was explicitly and unequivocally affirmed with many flattering remarks.[3] Quadratus, who seems to have succeeded Severus, was soon approached by a cautious Aristides for fresh confirmation of his immunity; Quadratus was pleased to oblige.[4] From that time Aristides was at last secure in his ἀτέλεια. What is notable about his many tribulations is that the immunity had been so difficult to obtain, requiring the support of the emperor and many important friends, and that various officials had paid so little attention to exemptions already granted and indeed to Aristides' own wishes. The impression derived from an examination of the legal texts earlier—that every obstacle was put in the way of immunity grants to wealthy rhetors, not to mention philosophers—is fully borne out by the case of Aristides.

Several other relevant instances are to hand, although there is nowhere the fullness of detail which exists for Aristides. Philostratus tells the story of a rhetorical contest in Rome before the emperor Septimius Severus: Apollonius of Athens was the victor over Heracleides of Lycia. The result was that the emperor deprived Heracleides of his ἀτέλεια.[5] Similarly the emperor Caracalla stripped Philiscus, professor at Athens, of his ἀτέλεια: Philostratus describes the scene in which Philiscus claimed that immunity belonged to any incumbent of the chair at Athens. Caracalla shouted in reply, 'Neither you nor any other teacher is immune. Not for miserable little speeches would I deprive cities of men who will perform liturgies.'[6] The

---

[1] Aristid. 50. 88 Keil.   [2] Aristid. 50. 92 Keil.
[3] Aristid. 50. 92–3 Keil.   [4] Aristid. 50. 63 ff. Keil.
[5] *VS*, p. 601.   [6] *VS*, p. 623.

apparent ease with which Septimius Severus and Caracalla in these cases revoked immunities again suggests the insecurity and impermanence of any such grant. The petulant and extravagant remark of Caracalla implies full awareness of the economic dangers of exempting sophists who were rich.

As emperors could revoke immunity, so naturally they could bestow it. Favorinus had tried to obtain it from Hadrian; Aristides was offered appeal to Rome. We happen to know that Marcus granted ἀτέλεια to the sophist Hadrian and that Caracalla granted it to Philostratus of Lemnos when (as the biographer Philostratus points out) the sophist was only twenty-four years old.[1] Further, a valuable inscription records a confirmation of immunity for Claudius Rufinus of Smyrna by Septimius Severus and Caracalla jointly.[2] It appears that in spite of an immunity Rufinus had in the past served his city as στρατηγός, voluntarily but under pressure;[3] Severus and Caracalla declare that henceforth he should be left undisturbed. Presumably the Smyrnaeans, ignoring his immunity, had tried again to exploit Rufinus—one is reminded of Aristides—and there had been an appeal to Rome. The inscription makes reference to the immunity enactments pertaining to sophists.[4] It seems clear enough that Rufinus had not been enrolled by the Smyrnaeans among the limited number of authorized exempted rhetors and that his claim consisted in being ἄγαν ἐπιστήμων as well as (probably) practising in a city not his own.

The present chapter began with the problem of reconciling special privileges made available for distinguished persons with the needs of the provincial cities where they would normally serve as magistrates and undertake various liturgies. The extant evidence on this problem suggests that the potential dangers inherent in honorific immunities were recognized and, after the short-lived liberality of Hadrian's edict, averted by making it difficult for any rhetor or philosopher of means to claim the immunity to which he might theoretically be

---

[1] Ibid.   [2] *IGR* 4. 1402 = *SIG*³ 876.

[3] Ibid.: ὑμῶν (the Smyrnaeans) ἑκουσίῳ ἀνάγκῃ προκαλουμένων.

[4] Ibid.: τὴν προκειμένην τοῖς σοφισταῖς κατὰ τὰς θείας τῶν προγόνων ἡμῶν διατάξεις ἀτέλειαν τῶν λειτουργιῶν καρπούμενος.

entitled. The forbidding wit of Hadrian's reply to Favorinus, together with the parallel phrasing in Pius' edict, and the limitation of exemptions to fixed numbers within each city put widespread immunities beyond possibility; and it will not be forgotten that the local βουλή supplied the list of exempted professional persons. As far as one can tell, no important and wealthy rhetor is known ever to have received immunity as one of the statutorily permitted number in a city. Those who did will have been lesser men whose absence from magistracies and liturgies cannot have been much missed. The provisions for immunity beyond the fixed number were vague enough for claims to be contested, and even when grants were made they were not taken by the provincials as serious deterrents to their imposing new burdens on a man who had at one time been immune. The cavalier cancellation of ἀτέλεια by emperors implies an insecurity in the grant; and the direct involvement of emperors in the bestowal of it, whether in person or by letter, shows that grants beyond the number were not made lightly.

In the second and early third centuries the majority of important sophists were pleased to improve their status and prestige through service and donations, and the availability or —doubtless in some cases—the possession of honorific immunity was of no concern to them except that voluntary benefactions had more lustre than compulsory ones. But there were some who really wanted to have immunity: the legal machinery was so devised that exemptions could be the most difficult to claim for those who mattered the most.

IV

SOPHISTS AND EMPERORS

THE wealth, intelligence, and patriotism of the sophists, expressed in public service and benefaction, contributed largely to the prosperity of their cities. They became a valuable part of the local administration which was so important to the efficient functioning of the Roman empire. Since teachers and rhetors had tended the affairs of eastern cities long before the second century, it was no accident that as the rhetors became more numerous, more important, and richer, their cities did too. Hence the resurgence of places like Pergamum and Ephesus. The social and political influence of the rhetors of the late republic and early empire can be discerned clearly by anyone who cares to look; in the second century it simply cannot be missed, so conspicuous are the intellectual and (in many cases) lineal descendants of those earlier men of culture.

In the two centuries before the advent of the Second Sophistic the activities of the litterati regularly included service on embassies to powerful Roman officials and aristocrats, whose personal acquaintance with the envoys was often the cause of special favours to the cities they represented. And in some cases eastern confidants and advisers can be recognized in the entourage of generals and emperors. One recalls the embassies of Potamo to Julius Caesar and Augustus, the intercession of Theopompus with Caesar on behalf of Cnidos, the association of Theophanes of Mytilene with Pompey, or the presence of Strabo in Egypt with the prefect Aelius Gallus.[1] It is necessary to bear this earlier history in mind when approaching the second century and the Greek renaissance,

[1] On Potamo, Theopompus, and Theophanes, see Bowersock, *Augustus and the Greek World* (1965), ch. I. On Aelius Gallus, *PIR²*, A 179 and Bowersock, op. cit., pp. 128–9 (cf. G. V. Sumner, *Phoenix* 21 [1967], 133).

since what we regularly identify with the Second Sophistic already existed in embryo. Augustus' employment of Athenodorus of Tarsus and Pompeius Macer adumbrates the imperial posts of the sophists in Philostratus;[1] and similarly do the careers of Ti. Claudius Balbillus, *ad responsa graeca* and later prefect of Egypt, or Dionysius of Alexandria, *ab epistulis* to Nero and others.[2] The Roman empire became increasingly a Graeco-Roman unity: the role of literate easterners did not essentially change throughout that development which it helped to effect, but their role became far more prominent.

The relations between the sophists and the Roman emperors illustrate at every point the continuity of the diplomatic tradition of personal contact, advice, and intercession. One of the early representatives of the Second Sophistic movement (as such) was the Flavian sophist Scopelian of Smyrna, who is said to have gone on many embassies to the emperor: one of these concerned the celebrated vine edict of Domitian.[3] Scopelian was dispatched to Rome as ambassador not merely of Smyrna but, according to Philostratus, of all Asia.[4] One supposes that he was the chosen delegate of the Koinon, of which Scopelian, like his paternal ancestors, served as high priest.[5] The embassy about the vines was attended by a great success. Scopelian was honoured by Domitian, and disciples followed him back to Asia. The oration to the emperor was still celebrated and read in the early third century.[6]

Toward the end of his life, at a time when Smyrna required an embassy on matters of great import, Scopelian found himself too old to travel, and the task fell to a new and young sophist, Polemo, who had never before served as envoy.[7] Like Scopelian, Polemo came from a distinguished Ionian family which was well known not only to the citizens of Asia but also to emperors and Roman aristocrats.[8] The choice of Polemo

[1] Athenodorus and Macer: Bowersock, op. cit., ch. III.

[2] Balbillus: *PIR²*, C 813 and H.-G. Pflaum, *Les Carrières procuratoriennes équestres* (1960) i, no. 15, pp. 34–41. Dionysius: *PIR²*, D 103 and Pflaum, op. cit., p. 684, n. 1.

[3] *VS*, p. 520. Cf. Suet. *Dom.* 7. 2, 14. 2; Statius, *Silv.* iv. 3. 11 ff.

[4] *VS*, p. 520.

[5] *VS*, p. 515. Cf. A. Stein, *Epitymbion H. Swoboda dargebracht* (1927), p. 303.

[6] Cf. the testimony of Philostratus, *VS*, p. 520.

[7] *VS*, p. 521.   [8] Bowersock, op. cit., pp. 143–4.

was in every respect sensible, even predictable. This eloquent
ambassador served many times afterwards on missions to the
emperor; and we are told that at a time when Hadrian's
favour was directed rather to Ephesus, Polemo so converted
him to Smyrna that he was moved to bestow ten million drach-
mas upon the city. With those funds a corn market, a gymnasium, and a temple were built.[1] There exists an inscription
from Smyrna which testifies to the effectiveness of Polemo with
the emperor Hadrian: it refers to what was obtained from the
emperor διὰ Ἀντωνίου Πολέμωνος.[2] This is explicit, official,
and contemporary documentation of Philostratus' account of
Polemo as an ambassador. The voice of Polemo was powerful even from the grave. He had been appointed ambassador
on a matter of temple rights in Smyrna, but unfortunately his
death prevented a personal appearance before the emperor.
Yet the emperor, who will by now have been Antoninus Pius,
demanded to hear the speech which Polemo had composed for
the occasion, and on the strength of that posthumous appeal
the embassy had a successful outcome.[3]

The ailing Aristides went to Rome only once, when he
delivered the multitude of commonplaces which make up his
address to Rome.[4] He was nevertheless able to use his influence
and skill as a sophist in the interest of Smyrna by intercession
with Marcus Aurelius and Commodus. And indeed, as Aristides himself realized, he owed some service to the city in view
of his persistent and unorthodox refusals in the past to hold any
public office or undertake any liturgy.[5] An earthquake laid
Smyrna in ruins in 178: such an event was always an occasion
for an embassy to the emperor. Funds had to be acquired for the
costly business of rebuilding, and therefore Smyrna dispatched
to Marcus and Commodus some unknown representatives.
Although avoiding the journey to Rome, Aristides composed

---

[1] VS, p. 531.   [2] IGR 4. 1431, l. 33.   [3] VS, p. 540.
[4] Aristid. 26 Keil (εἰς 'Ρώμην). Cf. 48. 60 Keil (on the journey to Rome).
Cf. J. H. Oliver, The Ruling Power (1953), pp. 886–7; also for an account of
what may be Aristides' original contribution in the speech, J. Bleicken, NGA
(1966) 7, pp. 264–5. C. A. Behr, Aelius Aristides and the Sacred Tales (1968),
pp. 88–90, argues that the εἰς 'Ρώμην was delivered in 155 on a second visit to
Rome (for which, however, evidence is wanting).
[5] See Aristid. 20 Keil.

a letter to the emperors in which he recalled his meeting
with them two years before, when they were both in the East.
The appeal of Aristides survives.[1] It is not excessively long, and
it cannot be denied a certain contrived power. The sophist
conjured up an affecting picture of Smyrna, the glory of Asia,
transformed into a wasteland.[2] Aristides' appeal was successful, and the emperors had already sent off assistance to Smyrna
before the formal embassy even arrived to make its request.
Aristides was justifiably proud of what he had done for his
city without even leaving Asia; and when, after the accession
of Commodus, a rumour reached him that the new emperor
was planning another visit to the East, he wrote to urge the
desirability of an imperial return to Smyrna to behold the city
rising again from the dust. This proposal of Aristides to Commodus constitutes his latest surviving work,[3] a fitting indication
of the terms on which a senior sophist felt he could approach
the ruler of the world.

Other examples of diplomatic activity can be found in the
extant materials, although one lacks the engaging details
which exist for men like Polemo or Aristides. For instance, it is
known that Hadrian much admired Marcus of Byzantium as
a result of an appeal for his city on an embassy;[4] and Alexander the Clay-Plato appeared before Pius on behalf of his native
Cilician Seleuceia.[5] Apollonius of Athens went to Rome to
speak before Septimius Severus,[6] and Heliodorus the sophist
made a profound impression upon Caracalla by pleading his
case alone when his colleague had fallen ill.[7]

These lesser embassies serve to reinforce the view of sophistic
diplomacy already documented by the fuller accounts. The
sophists were in a unique position to gain the ear and sym-
pathy of the emperor, and it was in their power thereby to
enhance the prestige, beauty, and affluence of their chosen
cities. Through their lavish benefactions cities like Smyrna
and Ephesus were substantially helped to reach a new level of

[1] Aristid. 19 Keil.
[2] Ibid., 2: ἃ νῦν πάντα ἐν κόνει. On Aristides' meeting with the emperors in
the East, see VS, pp. 582–3.
[3] Aristid. 21 Keil. Cf. Behr, op. cit., pp. 113–14, for an argument in favour of
a proconsul, not Commodus, as the addressee.
[4] VS, p. 530.   [5] VS, p. 570.   [6] VS, p. 601.   [7] VS, p. 626.

prosperity; but it is clear that not only could a sophist like Polemo himself present Smyrna with fine buildings, but he could also elicit still more for the city by virtue of his relationship with the emperor. Similarly in times of crisis, such as the aftermath of an earthquake, the high connections of sophists could produce rapid aid. The economic importance of the greater sophists was thus double, in that they could both provide and secure money for the cities.

The situation was not different, it must be added, for persons like the Vedii Antonini of Ephesus. The father and son of that name in the first half of the second century are not known to have been sophists, though they were doubtless men of superior education; but their huge benefactions to the city were on a sophistic scale, and a recent inscription attests their presence on embassies to Roman emperors.[1] The father Vedius will have appeared before Trajan and Hadrian, while the son was on good terms with Pius, Marcus, and Lucius Verus. One text even provides the welcome information that Vedius was responsible for the reception of Lucius Verus in Ephesus on the journey east in 162.[2] The activities of the Ephesian Vedii offer a parallel to those of the sophists, but more than that. It will be recalled that the younger Vedius' daughter was the wife of the celebrated sophist Damian, and thus the parallel with the sophists became a link—a link which produced three consuls and two brides of consuls in the next generation.[3]

The personal friendships which subsisted in the later republic and early empire between literary men from the East and eminent Romans had their counterparts in the age of the Second Sophistic. The relationship had always been—and remained—advisory in at least one of its aspects. So it was, for example, in the case of Dio of Prusa and Trajan, the philosophic counsellor and his emperor; so it had been with Athenodorus and Augustus. It is not necessary to believe the anecdote which Philostratus tells of Dio and Trajan riding together in

---

[1] See above, p. 28. The embassies: *JÖAI* 44 (1959), Beibl., cols. 257–9, ll. 10–12 (father), 18–20 (son). For the relation of Vedius' activity to the Asian proconsulate of L. Antonius Albus, cf. G. W. Bowersock, *HSCP* 72 (1968), 289 ff.

[2] *JÖAI* (n. 1 above), ll. 22–9.

[3] See the stemma in *PIR²*, Pars III, p. 178; also above, p. 28, n. 6.

a golden chariot: Dio is speaking in Greek, and Trajan remarks to him, 'I know not what you are saying, but I love you as myself.'[1] The relationship implied by this story is credible anyhow.

Trajan was also a friend to Polemo, to whom he granted the privilege of free travel wherever he wished.[2] Hadrian, another admirer of Polemo, extended that privilege to the sophist's posterity and added others; his great-grandson, Hermocrates, is found fully equipped with privileges of all sorts.[3] Hadrian's relations with Polemo are well illustrated by the emperor's own admission that his final statement on the affairs of the whole empire (a *breviarium totius imperii*, one supposes) was prepared with Polemo's advice.[4] Nor is this the only indication of Hadrian's regard: his invitation to that sophist to deliver the oration at the consecration of the Olympieum at Athens was perhaps an embarrassing repudiation of the obvious person for the occasion, Herodes Atticus.[5] Polemo's enemies at Smyrna had once tried to compromise him by allegations that he was spending on himself funds transmitted by the emperor for the good of the city, but Hadrian replied firmly with a letter declaring that Polemo had rendered him an account of the moneys which he had given the city.[6] Not that the great sophist did not spend extravagantly for his own ostentation. He could be seen travelling along the roads of Asia in a chariot with silver bridles and an elaborate entourage of pack-animals, horses, slaves, and dogs.[7] But Philostratus rightly observed that such a display gave lustre to a city no less than a fine agora or a splendid array of buildings, 'for not only does a city give a man renown, but a city itself acquires it from a man'.[8]

The story of Polemo's expulsion of the future Antoninus Pius from his house is well known.[9] It happened when Pius was serving as proconsul of Asia, and it illustrates the sophist's pride and social eminence. Either with or without the efforts

---

[1] *VS*, p. 488.   [2] *VS*, p. 532.   [3] *VS*, p. 532, cf. p. 611.
[4] *VS*, p. 534: ἐν ταῖς ὑπὲρ τῆς βασιλείας διαθήκαις. Note also Polemo's travels with Hadrian: Appendix II below.
[5] *VS*, p. 533. Cf. P. Graindor, *Un Milliardaire antique: Hérode Atticus et sa famille* (1930), pp. 45, 58.
[6] *VS*, p. 533.   [7] *VS*, p. 532.   [8] Ibid.
[9] *VS*, p. 534. See above p. 23.

of Hadrian to effect a reconciliation Polemo did not suffer at the accession of Pius.

But we happen to know that the young Marcus Aurelius was not much impressed by him in the year 143 (he set down his views in a letter to Fronto);[1] and Marcus' opinion may have something to do with another interesting personal relationship, namely that between himself and the rival of Polemo, Herodes Atticus. It is one of the oddities of the correspondence with Fronto that the teacher of Marcus had somehow not discovered (at least by 140) the cordial ties between his pupil and Herodes. For Herodes had once spent some time in the house of Calvisius Ruso, grandfather of Marcus.[2] Fronto was preparing, in the reign of Pius, to attack Herodes in court, and Marcus begged him to observe the friendship he felt for the great sophist.[3] It is not very astonishing to find Fronto at a later date considering himself also a good friend of Herodes—so powerful was an expression of princely favour.[4] The relations between Marcus and Herodes were not smooth throughout, but they endured. It is known that in his first appointments of professors at Athens Marcus took the advice of Herodes.[5] One can deduce that over many decades the two men corresponded: some years after an awkward business in which Herodes had been obliged to defend himself before Marcus in Pannonia against charges made by his enemies at Athens, Herodes wrote to Marcus to ask why the emperor no longer corresponded with him. In the past Marcus had often written as many as three letters a day.[6]

Like Herodes, Aristides claimed to have been a regular correspondent with emperors,[7] and as a result of the visit of

[1] Fronto, p. 29 van den Hout: *videtur mihi agricola strenuus, summa sollertia praeditus* . . .

[2] Fronto, p. 37 van den Hout. The date of this letter, normally given as the early 140s, is not altogether clear, depending on a trial in which Fronto was planning to speak ill of Herodes. See below, pp. 93–9. On P. Calvisius Tullus Ruso (*cos.* 109) see R. Syme, *Tacitus* (1958), ii. 793, item 7.

[3] Fronto, loc. cit. (preceding note).

[4] Fronto, p. 106 and p. 130 van den Hout: *Herodes summus nunc meus.*

[5] *VS*, p. 566 (for chairs of Platonic, Stoic, Peripatetic, and Epicurean philosophy).

[6] *VS*, p. 562. On the scene in Pannonia, *VS*, pp. 560–1 (see below p. 98).

[7] Aristid. 42. 14 Keil. For Marcus and Aristides, cf. R. Pack, *CP* 42 (1947), 17 f.

Marcus and Commodus in 176 he could point to visible manifestations of his intimacy with the mighty. It is hard to believe
that the emperor derived much pleasure from Aristides'
company; but evidently he was prepared to attend promptly
to Aristides' requests, and that, after all, was what really
mattered.

For many sophists whose advice was sought, and whose
company was congenial, emperors found official posts in the
court at Rome and in the entourage in provinces. In the second
and early third centuries the office of *ab epistulis* for Greek
correspondence is found to have been monopolized by eastern
Greek sophists and rhetors. Between the reigns of Hadrian and
Caracalla twelve oriental litterati can be distinguished as *ab
epistulis*, and that is a substantial number.[1] In most instances
the precise designation of the post is *ab epistulis graecis*, although
not all the sources (notably allusions in Philostratus) are so
explicit. One scholar has argued that the post of *ab epistulis* was
not split into Latin and Greek divisions under Hadrian, as
previously thought, but under Marcus.[2] This may be so; the
evidence is inadequate. And it is a fact, however it has to be
explained, that the title of Valerius Eudaemon under Hadrian
was incontrovertibly *ab epistulis graecis*.[3]

In some instances the post *ab epistulis* constituted the first
step in an equestrian or ultimately senatorial career for a cultivated Greek. In other cases it was quite clearly no more
than a way to retain a man at the court without guarantee of
advancement in the civil service. It is remarkable, however,
that of the two Greek *ab epistulis* known from the reign of
Hadrian both became prefect of Egypt and both are reported
to have incurred at some point the emperor's wrath. They are
C. Avidius Heliodorus and Valerius Eudaemon.

Heliodorus was a Syrian rhetor, father of the rebel Avidius
Cassius and friend to Aelius Aristides.[4] It is known from Cassius Dio that he was *ab epistulis* under Hadrian, and he is

---

[1] Cf. H.-G. Pflaum, *Les Carrières procuratoriennes équestres* (1960), ii. 684, n. 1;
G. B. Townend, 'The Post of *Ab Epistulis* in the second century', *Historia* 10
(1961), 375–81, with a list on pp. 380–1. Cf. F. Millar, *JRS* 57 (1967), 16.

[2] Townend, op. cit.

[3] *ILS* 1449. Cf. Pflaum, op. cit., i, no. 110, pp. 264–71.

[4] *PIR²*, A 1405.

established as Egyptian prefect before the death of Hadrian.[1] It was a spectacular elevation, clouded only by the report of the Augustan History that Hadrian attacked Heliodorus in a notorious letter.[2] It would be perverse to regard this Heliodorus as a philosopher distinct from the rhetor. Admittedly, the Augustan History designates the object of Hadrian's attack as a philosopher, but from an item in Cassius Dio one may conjecture philosophical activity on the part of the rhetor Heliodorus.[3] A philosopher-rhetor should evoke no surprise.

As for the Eudaemon against whom Hadrian raged, he was the *ab epistulis* who subsequently emerges as prefect of Egypt in the earlier part of Pius' reign.[4] Since Eudaemon did not reach the prefecture while Hadrian was still alive, it is perhaps easier to credit that he had some difficulty with that emperor. At any rate there is no disputing one scholar's opinion that Eudaemon's career suggests that he was an eminent man of letters.[5]

The puzzling relationship of Heliodorus and Eudaemon to the emperor Hadrian is not an isolated problem in the study of that intellectual monarch, and it may be profitable to linger for a moment on this issue. There are other literary men who present difficulties, namely Favorinus and Dionysius of Miletus. Favorinus quarrelled with Hadrian, yet lived.[6] No one would have guessed, until a papyrus turned up, that Favorinus had been exiled, although Cassius Dio does say that Hadrian *tried* to overthrow him.[7] If he was exiled, Hadrian

---

[1] Cf. A. Stein, *Die Präfekten von Aegypten* (1950), p. 73; O. Reinmuth, *Bulletin of the American Society of Papyrologists* 4 (1967), 95.

[2] *HA* Hadr. 15. 5: *Heliodorum famosis litteris lacessivit.*

[3] *HA* Hadr. 16. 10 alludes to *Epictetum et Heliodorum philosophos.* But observe Dio 69. 3. 5 in which the Milesian Dionysius taunts Avidius Heliodorus, the *ab epistulis*: Καῖσαρ χρήματα μέν σοι καὶ τιμὴν δοῦναι δύναται, ῥήτορα δέ σε ποιῆσαι οὐ δύναται. Heliodorus will have wished to be (like those men in Philostratus, above pp. 10 ff.) a philosopher who excelled also in rhetoric. The Heliodorus of *HA* Hadr. 16. 5 and 10 is identified as C. Avidius Heliodorus in *PIR*², A 1405 (A. Stein).

[4] H.-G. Pflaum, *Les Carrières procuratoriennes équestres* (1960), i, no. 110, pp. 264–71; A. Stein, *Die Präfekten von Aegypten* (1950), pp. 74–6; O. Reinmuth, *Bulletin of the American Society of Papyrologists* 4 (1967), 96.

[5] Pflaum, op. cit., i. 271: 'un homme de lettres réputé'.

[6] *VS*, p. 489.

[7] Dio 69. 3. 4: καταλύειν ἐπεχείρει. On the papyrus *De Exilio* and its problems see above p. 36.

must have done it. But when? At the end of the reign, perhaps. Philostratus' report of the Athenians' overturning a bronze statue of Favorinus could belong not—as he says it does—to the aftermath of an immunity appeal:[1] Favorinus certainly abandoned that appeal, and it therefore seems hardly sufficient justification for the Athenians' action.

In the case of Dionysius of Miletus, Dio produces the odd report that Hadrian tried to overthrow him too, along with Favorinus.[2] Yet Philostratus signals specially Hadrian's favour to Dionysius and mentions that the emperor appointed him satrap of eminent peoples, an item which was confirmed and clarified by the discovery of an inscription at Ephesus identifying him as a procurator.[3] Is Dio's report totally muddled, or has he preserved some intimation of an unpleasant fact? The existence of the Favorinus papyrus has forced disquieting reflections about Hadrian and the sophists.

To summarize, in four cases (those of Heliodorus, Eudaemon, Favorinus, and Dionysius) there is reason to assume the emperor's favour *and* his hostility. Possibly in those last desperate years that saw the suicide of Servianus and other unpleasantness Hadrian turned upon certain of the greater sophists.[4] With them one could subjoin the historian Arrian, abandoning Rome in the last years of Hadrian's life after a brilliant career under that very emperor.[5] There remains a difficulty: Heliodorus was installed as prefect of Egypt before Hadrian died, but perhaps not long before. And he remained in office for several years under Pius, to be followed directly by another fallen sophist, Valerius Eudaemon. The

---

[1] *VS*, p. 490. Since Speech 37 in the corpus of Dio of Prusa is commonly accepted as the work of Favorinus (cf. A. Barigazzi, *Opere: Favorino di Arelate* [1966], pp. 298 ff.), it is relevant to note that the speech is devoted to reproaching the Corinthians for removal of a bronze statue which they had erected in the speaker's honour.

[2] Dio 69. 3. 4.

[3] *VS*, p. 524: σατράπην . . . οὐκ ἀφανῶν ἐθνῶν. The inscription: J. Keil, *JÖAI* 40 (1953), 6, ἐπίτροπον τοῦ Σεβαστοῦ, probably of a province of middling importance. Keil proposed Raetia.

[4] On Hadrian's last years, see R. Syme, *Tacitus* (1958), ii. 600–1, and H.-G. Pflaum, *Historia-Augusta Colloquium Bonn 1963* (1964), pp. 91 ff.

[5] *PIR²*, F 219. Arrian was consul in 128 or 129, subsequently legate of Cappadocia. Under the Antonines he evidently lived in Athens, where he was archon in 145/6.

conflicting reports about Hadrian and the sophists may have some basis in Hadrian's behaviour and character, and also in the influence of other people than the emperor. There may yet be more to be known or postulated about the last months of Hadrian's life.

To return to the *ab epistulis graecis*. Aelius Aristides alludes to one Celer, an imperial secretary under Hadrian or Antoninus Pius (or both).[1] This will certainly be a man of the same name known from Philostratus as a lifelong enemy of Dionysius of Miletus and identified also as an imperial secretary, a good one.[2] It is not so easy to say whether this rhetor is the teacher of Marcus Aurelius, Caninius Celer, but nothing stands against it.[3] Things of this kind can be expected: a cultivated Greek at the court serving as pedagogue. One is reminded of Nestor of Tarsus long before Celer or again of Antipater of Hierapolis after him.[4] (Antipater held precisely the post of *ab epistulis* and was the tutor of Caracalla and Geta.) Aid in reconstructing the career of Celer comes from an unexpected source, the account in Dio of Hadrian's attempts to overthrow Favorinus and Dionysius; Dio says that Hadrian tried to elevate their enemies.[5] Now the possibility of Dio's preserving a genuine report of a reversal of Hadrian's opinion has been canvassed in the light of other evidence. It is not impossible. The chronology is perfect for a suggestion that sometime in his last years Hadrian appointed Celer *ab epistulis*. Celer was, we know, roughly a contemporary of Dionysius and his sworn enemy. From Aristides it can be inferred that he was holding his secretarial post early under Pius; a similar conclusion follows from an identification with the teacher of Marcus. Hence perhaps still more evidence on Hadrian and the sophists at the end of his reign.

Two *ab epistulis* are known from the reign of Marcus, both from the latter part of it and both clearly eastern Greeks. The first was Alexander the Clay-Plato from Cilician Seleuceia, who was summoned by Marcus to Pannonia and given the

[1] Aristid. 50. 57 Keil.　　　　　　　　　　　　[2] *VS*, p. 524.
[3] Marcus Aurelius, *Ad se ipsum* 8. 25. Cf. *HA* Marcus 2. 4, Ver. 2. 5.
[4] On Nestor, Bowersock, *Augustus and the Greek World* (1965), pp. 34–5. On Antipater, see below, pp. 55 f.
[5] Dio 69. 3. 4.

secretarial post.[1] The second is a man of whom we have only recently learned more, Ti. Claudius Vibianus Tertullus. This person turned up on a bilingual inscription from Ephesus as *ab epistulis graecis, a rationibus Augustorum*, and *praefectus vigilum*.[2] Although initially assigned a Severan date, Tertullus has recently emerged as *ab epistulis graecis* under Marcus, precisely between the years 172 and 175.[3] He was a servant of Asclepius and recipient of honours bestowed by the city of Pergamum.[4] We may suppose him to be a native Pergamene. With Tertullus placed securely in the reign of Marcus between 172 and 175, it is not impossible that he was successor to Alexander the Clay-Plato. And a further important suggestion presents itself: Tertullus' post *a rationibus Augustorum* indicates tenure under Marcus and Commodus, with the *praefectura vigilum* left to be dated to the reign of Commodus. There is no warrant to call Vibianus Tertullus a sophist, but his qualifications will undoubtedly have included some kind of rhetorical or literary proficiency.

Each new item permits greater clarity and coherence in the picture of sophists and rhetors in the imperial service. The new Tertullus evidence is a great help; it can even be serviceable in determining his successor. The grammarian Phrynichus dedicated his work on Attic diction to a Cornelianus as royal secretary.[5] Phrynichus flourished under Commodus, and there is reason to view him as a rival of Pollux for the emperor's patronage.[6] The *ab epistulis* Cornelianus is not otherwise known, but Phrynichus does make an interesting comment about Cornelianus' appointment. The flattery is extravagant: he was appointed, Phrynichus declares, to superintend Greek

---

[1] *VS*, p. 571.

[2] *ILS* 1344. Cf. *PIR²*, C 1049 and H.-G. Pflaum, *Les Carrières procuratoriennes équestres* (1960), no. 252, pp. 683–4. The discussion of this text by G. B. Townend in *Historia* 10 (1961), 377 is now out of date in view of the new inscription cited in the following note.

[3] This is the testimony of a new inscription in the Asclepieum at Pergamum. Although not completely published, it is quoted in part by H.-G. Pflaum, op. cit., iii. 992: ἐπὶ ἐπιστολῶν Ἑλληνικῶν Αὐτοκράτορος Καίσαρος Μ. Αὐρηλίου Ἀντωνείνου Σεβαστοῦ Γερμανικοῦ. The date is guaranteed by Marcus' titulature.

[4] Ibid.

[5] Phrynichus, Ἐκλογὴ ῥημάτων καὶ ὀνομάτων Ἀττικῶν.

[6] The *floruit* of Phrynichus can be had from the dedication of his Σοφιστικὴ παρασκευή to the emperor Commodus. On Pollux, *VS*, pp. 592–3.

affairs by the emperors of the Romans (οἱ Ῥωμαίων βασιλεῖς), who by giving him the title of secretary in fact chose him as a partner in their rule.[1] Who were the βασιλεῖς that appointed Cornelianus? It can be said with assurance that Tertullus was *ab epistulis* of Marcus in the first half of the 170s, and that his next post was *a rationibus* of Marcus and Commodus jointly. Thus there was a vacancy in the secretarial post during the joint rule. Cornelianus was appointed by οἱ Ῥωμαίων βασιλεῖς and Phrynichus can be associated with Commodus' reign. Let it be stated, therefore, that Tertullus was succeeded by Cornelianus. The βασιλεῖς were Marcus and Commodus.

If Cornelianus' tenure lasted into the reign of Commodus (there is not yet any reason to assume it did not), he will be one of the few *ab epistulis graecis* known from the reign. A certain Larichus is attested in that office for *c.* 186,[2] and it is, to be sure, attested that Commodus appointed the sophist Hadrian to the post with apologies for not having done so earlier.[3] The appointment came too late since the sophist lay ill; it is generally and correctly supposed that he cannot have served for long, if at all. The sophist's connections with the Ummidii Quadrati might not have made him altogether welcome to Commodus.[4] It will not be forgotten that early in the reign an Ummidius Quadratus was privy to a plot against that emperor.[5]

Under Severus, the sophist Aelius Antipater of Hierapolis cannot be missed. Passing early in the reign from the chair at Athens, where Philostratus may have heard him, Antipater

---

[1] Phrynichus, Ἐκλογή, p. 475 Rutherford.
[2] *AE* 1952. 6. Cf. J. H. Oliver, *Hesperia* 36 (1967), 332.
[3] *VS*, p. 590.
[4] There exist on stone from Ephesus some elegiac verses in which Hadrian the sophist honours Cn. Claudius Severus, cos. II in 173, who is described as father of an Ummidius Quadratus (it is unclear which). The identifications of Hadrian and Severus were made by E. Groag in *Wiener Studien* 24 (1902), 261 ff. and incorporated in *PIR²*, C 1024; the inscription is reprinted by J. Keil, with Groag's interpretation, in *JÖAI* 40 (1953), 14. None of these references is known to A. N. Sherwin-White, *The Letters of Pliny: A Social and Historical Commentary* (1966), pp. 431, 762, where the Hadrian of the inscription is assumed—as before Groag's article of 1902—to be the emperor and the Severus to be L. Catilius Severus, cos. II in 120.
[5] Dio 73. 4. 6; Herodian 1. 8. 4; *HA* Commod. 4. 1. On the Ummidii, see now R. Syme, *Historia* 17 (1968), 72 ff.

became an important figure in the court.¹ He persuaded the emperor to arrange an ill-starred marriage between his daughter and the great-grandson of Polemo, and he was himself the teacher of Severus' sons.² An inscription from Ephesus that can be dated between 200 and 205 records a reply of Caracalla to a legation from the Ephesians: it appears from that document that members of the prince's *consilium* included Aelius Antipater, 'my friend, teacher, and *ab epistulis*'.³ As Philostratus reveals, this favoured sophist had a glorious career after his service as *ab epistulis*, at least up to a point. Severus gave him consular rank and dispatched him as legate of Bithynia.⁴ However, he was dismissed from that magistracy for undue severity. By the time of the murder of Geta, Antipater was moved to compose a threnody on the subject for Caracalla, who cannot have liked the reproach.⁵ It was said by some that Antipater starved himself to death.⁶

Other sophistic *ab epistulis* can be identified, although little can be said about them. They clearly fit the established pattern. Maximus of Aegae and Aspasius of Ravenna, both Greek-speaking sophists known to Philostratus, are attested as secretaries, and there is also the Sempronius Aquila, *ab epistulis graecis* on a stone from Ancyra.⁷ Some connection with Philostratus' Aquila from Galatia is irresistible. That Aquila was a pupil of Chrestus of Byzantium, and Chrestus had been a pupil of Herodes.⁸

There had long been a connection between the legal profession and the sophists, a connection which arose naturally enough from the forensic activity of rhetors. The explicit testimony of Philostratus reveals the legal competence of Nicetes and Scopelian, as well as the legal character of the rhetoric of Antiochus and Damian. An inscription attests the

¹ *VS*, p. 607. See above, p. 53.
² *VS*, pp. 610–11 (the marriage); *VS*, p. 607 (tutor of Severus' sons, θεῶν διδάσκαλος).
³ *Forschungen in Ephesos* 2, no. 26, p. 126, ll. 18–19: Αἴλιος Ἀντίπατρος ὁ φίλος μου καὶ διδάσκαλος κ[αὶ τὴν σύντα]ξιν τῶν ἑλλη[νι]κῶν ἐπιστολῶν ἐπιτετραμμένος.
⁴ *VS*, p. 607.   ⁵ Ibid.   ⁶ Ibid.
⁷ Maximus of Aegae: Philostr. *Vit. Apoll.* 1. 3. 5 (cf. 1. 12. 14); Aspasius of Ravenna: *VS*, p. 628; Sempronius Aquila: *IGR* 3. 188.
⁸ *VS*, p. 591. Cf. A. R. Birley, *Britain and Rome: Essays pres. to E. Birley* (1966), pp. 58–60.

legal skill of Lollianus.[1] Conjunctions like νομικὸς καὶ ῥήτωρ are found on stone.[2] While the post of *ab epistulis* absorbed the largest number of rhetors and sophists, another office was especially suited to those legally minded, that of *advocatus fisci* either in a province or at Rome. Zeuxidemus, the father—as it seems—of the sophist Antipater appears as a provincial advocatus in Asia.[3] Similarly the sophist Quirinus, who, Philostratus says, attained great power through his position.[4] And the emperor Caracalla elevated the sophist Heliodorus (not to be confused with the Hadrianic rhetor) to the post of *advocatus fisci* at Rome.[5]

Discussion of certain of the *ab epistulis* whose careers went on from that post has already revealed the heights which some could reach. The prefecture of Egypt awaited Avidius Heliodorus and Valerius Eudaemon, the *praefectura vigilum* Vibianus Tertullus, and the legateship of Bithynia Aelius Antipater. Dionysius of Miletus became a procurator, and it is worth adding that the philosophic moralist Plutarch is said to have been a procurator.[6] One may appositely mention here the aspirations of a certain Diogenes of Amastris, as recorded by Philostratus: from childhood Diogenes was puffed up with dreams of satrapies, courts, and proximity to emperors.[7] 'Satrapy' was the very word Philostratus had used to describe the procuratorship of Dionysius of Miletus.[8]

The mightiest of the second-century sophists are not, of course, to be found in the lists of *ab epistulis*. Theirs was the

---

[1] *VS*, pp. 511, 516 (Nicetes); p. 519 (Scopelian); p. 569 (Antiochus); p. 606 (Damian). For Lollianus: *IG* ii/iii². 4211.

[2] See W. Kunkel, *Herkunft und soziale Stellung der römischen Juristen* (1952), p. 360.

[3] *IGR* 4. 819. On Zeuxidemus, see above, p. 22.   [4] *VS*, p. 621.

[5] *VS*, p. 626: Caracalla appointed him ὡς ἐπιτηδειότερον δικαστηρίοις καὶ δίκαις.

[6] Euseb. apud Syncell., p. 659 Dindorf: cf. E. Groag, *Die römischen Reichsbeamten von Achaia von Augustus bis auf Diokletian* (1939), pp. 145–7 and H.-G. Pflaum, *Les Carrières procuratoriennes équestres* (1961), iii. 1071. The protest of Latte (*apud* Ziegler, *P–W* 21. 1. 659) against the evidence of a procuratorship is worthless: he argued that Achaea was not governed by a procurator in Plutarch's time and therefore that Eusebius had to be wrong. Latte evidently did not know of the existence of non-governing procurators, nor did he know (though he could have) the work of Groag.

[7] *VS*, p. 592: σατραπείας, αὐλάς, καὶ τὸ ἄγχου βασιλέων ἐστήξειν.

[8] *VS*, p. 524. Cf. above, p. 52, n. 3.

grander destiny of powerful influence with emperors and personal prestige such as Polemo, Herodes, or Aristides enjoyed.
The consulate was always a possibility, as in the case of
Herodes Atticus. But the greatest service these men could
render the imperial regime was to preside over the factions
and finances of the eastern cities. Hadrian adroitly exploited
Herodes in Asia by appointing him corrector of the *civitates
liberae* in the days when the future Pius was proconsul.[1] It is in
the houses of the greatest sophists that the most spectacular
penetration of the senatorial order can be seen—not only
Herodes' consulate in 143 but that of Polemo's relative, M.
Antonius Zeno, in 148, or the five children of Damian and
Vedia who either became consuls or married them.[2]

In an age which had a strong taste for the artificial brilliance of the sophists, the role which they had had for centuries
in society and politics became conspicuous and stunning. The
Graeco-Roman οἰκουμένη permitted them to have international
prestige; and as in the old days the rhetors had associated in
official and unofficial relationships with the leaders of the
Roman aristocracy, so now they are found in similar relationships with the monarchs of the Roman empire. It could be
argued without apology that the Second Sophistic has more
importance in Roman History than it has in Greek Literature.

[1] *VS*, pp. 537, 548; cf. 554.   [2] See above, p. 28.

V

THE PRESTIGE OF GALEN

P LUTARCH reminded his readers once that in Homer a
doctor is valued more than many ordinary men,[1] and
at most times in human history those who could relieve
suffering and effect healing have enjoyed a special place in
society. The history of medicine is, in one of its aspects, a part
of the social history of a civilization. This has been true not
least of the debate over the availability of free medical service
in Greek and Roman antiquity.[2] The abundance, professionalism, and social standing of physicians seem often to vary
in direct proportion to the refinement of a culture, and that is
hardly surprising. In the classical world the connection between
progress in philosophy and literature and progress in medicine
is particularly obvious; one has only to reflect on the nearly
simultaneous activities of Socrates, Euripides, Hippocrates,
and Thucydides in the fifth century. Intellectual history is
always a complex fabric, and—what is more—it cannot and
must not be separated from the history of a society.

In the second century A.D. the doctor Galen acquired an
eminence and prestige among the aristocrats of Rome such as
no doctor before him. And the prestige of Galen continued
long after his death, but that is a different issue. It is not that
the essential feature of Galen's career, namely his service in the
court of the emperor, was anything new in the history of
doctors.[3] But the importance of his place in upper-class Roman
society was, as far as can be told, quite remarkable. There

[1] Plut. *De tuenda sanitate* 122 C, quoting Homer, *Iliad* xi. 514: πολλῶν ἀντάξιος
ἄλλων.
[2] Cf. L. Cohn-Haft, *The Public Physicians of Ancient Greece* (1956), p. 2,
n. 7, on A. G. Woodhead, 'The State Health Service in Ancient Greece',
Cambridge Historical Journal 10 (1952), 235 ff. (based on R. Pohl, *De graecorum
medicis publicis* [1905]).
[3] One may go back, for instance, to the celebrated Democedes of Croton
(Herod. 3. 125–37).

exists enough evidence to view the success of Galen within the context of the Graeco-Roman world of his time, and perhaps an effort to do so will provide a clearer understanding of many of the bizarre phenomena of the second century. It was not an accident that Galen emerged during the flowering of the so-called Second Sophistic movement.

To turn to Galen's career. Born in Pergamum in A.D. 129, he was the son of an architect by the name of Aelius Nico.[1] It is well to recall the extraordinary revival of Pergamum under the empire from the time when, as Aristides reveals, the god Asclepius summoned Julius Quadratus in the reign of Augustus to restore by his energy and benefactions the declining fortunes of the city.[2] For there are inscriptions which connect the father of Galen with the development of the new Pergamum:[3] an architect would, of course, have had an important role, and Nico seems to have worked on several great new buildings. In a dream he received advice to direct the studies of his son Galen to medicine and philosophy,[4] and so he did.

It is possible to collect from the vast writings which fill some twenty volumes in the old and standard edition of Galen a substantial and imposing list of his teachers in philosophy.[5] He says, moreover, that his first medical teacher was Satyrus, who was lecturing at Pergamum.[6] Galen's allusion to Satyrus is more meaningful than might initially appear, since the man is mentioned by Aelius Aristides, who encountered him at Pergamum during the course of his lingering illness.[7] Galen's attendance at the lectures of Satyrus will have occurred about the year 150: he tells us that this was the time when one Rufinus was building the great Asclepieum.[8] This Rufinus is

[1] *PIR²*, G 24. There is no ancient evidence for the *nomen* Claudius often attached to Galen in older scholarship. Even recent authors occasionally slip: J. H. Kent, *Corinth* viii. 3, *The Inscriptions* (1966), p. 85.

[2] See above p. 19.

[3] *IGR* 4. 503, 506. Cf. H. Hepding, *Philol.* 88 (1933), 100, n. 53.

[4] Galen 10. 609; 14. 608; 19. 43 Kühn (the last = 119 Mueller).

[5] The edition is that of Kühn. For references to Galen's philosophy teachers, see *PIR²*, G 24: they included Alexander of Damascus, Pelops Platonicus, Albinus Platonicus, Numisianus, and Eudemus the Peripatetic.

[6] Galen 19. 57 Kühn = 87 Mueller.   [7] Aristid. 49. 8 ff. Keil.

[8] Galen 2. 224 Kühn. The Greek transmitted is Κοστουνίου 'Ρουφίνου, clearly a confusion of Rufinus' *nomina*. On the identification and date, see Hepding, *Philol.* 88 (1933), 93 ff. Cf. *PIR²*, C 1637.

clearly none other than the Pergamene consular, L. Cuspius Pactumeius Rufinus, consul in 142; the Asclepieum he was building, even now accessible to tourists, was a well-known wonder in later antiquity and is several times alluded to as the ʿΡουφίνιον ἄλσος in Byzantine epigrams.[1] Now Rufinus, like Satyrus, was also known to Aristides, indeed—unlike Satyrus —he was a close personal friend (or so Aristides would have us believe).[2] It appears, therefore, that the testimony of Galen on his study at Pergamum at about the age of twenty can be correlated with the account of Aristides' sojourns at Pergamum in the same period; the protracted illness can be dated with virtual certainty to the decade 144–54.[3] Galen, perhaps through his father's position in Pergamum, seems, though a student, to have moved in elevated circles. The fact that he was in Pergamum at the same time as Aristides and had at least two acquaintances in common would be enough to prompt speculation that he met the great sophist himself, only twelve years his senior. Galen would have been interested to observe Aristides' hypochondria. It is good to have explicit evidence: an Arabic translation of a passage from Galen's Commentary on Plato's *Timaeus* provides a reference to Aristides. The passage is our only contemporary eyewitness report of the man: 'As for

[1] Notably in *Anth. Pal.* 9. 656, l. 14, where the enemy of Claudian is not to be understood: cf. Hepding, op. cit., 90 ff.

[2] Aristid. 50. 83–4, 107 Keil; *PIR*², C 1637.

[3] See A. Boulanger, *Aelius Aristide* (1923), pp. 465–8 and C. A. Behr, *Aelius Aristides and the Sacred Tales* (1968), Chaps. 2–4. The birth of Aristides can, from the configuration of the stars at the time (50. 57–8 Keil), be assigned to either 117 (perhaps early 118) or 129. (For October as the month, cf. O. Neugebauer and H. B. van Hoesen, *Greek Horoscopes* [1959], pp. 113–14; for 27 January 118, cf. Behr, loc. cit.) The right option is the earlier: M. Nonius Macrinus was proconsul of Asia when Aristides was 53 years old (Aristid. 22 Keil, subscription), and Macrinus' proconsulate belongs in 170/1 (cf. *Forschungen in Ephesos* 3. 29 and the consul on the Ostian Fasti for 154, M. N[onius Macrinus]). There is also Aristides' friendship with Avidius Heliodorus (50. 75 Keil), which probably developed when Aristides travelled in Egypt: Heliodorus was prefect there from 138 to 141 (Stein, *Die Präfekten von Aegypten* [1950], pp. 72–4). Cf. also D. Magie, *Roman Rule in Asia Minor* (1950) ii. 1492.

Recently J. H. Oliver, in his introduction to Aristides' *Panathenaicus* (*The Civilizing Power* [1968], p. 33), has accepted an argument of F. Lenz for a late birthdate of Aristides (*Rivista di cultura classica e medioevale* 5 [1963], 333). But Lenz's view is founded upon a misunderstanding of the end of the Athena hymn (37. 29 Keil): the βασιλεῖς in that passage are not Marcus and Verus but Zeus and Athena.

those', says Galen, 'whose souls are strong by nature and whose bodies are weak, I have seen only a few. One of them was Aristides from Mysia, and this man was one of the most outstanding orators. So it happened that lifelong activity in talking and declaiming caused his whole body to fade away.'[1] The meeting of Galen and Aristides, the doctor and the sophist, is an apt illustration of the age.

For his studies Galen travelled widely. He can be discovered in such academic centres as Smyrna, Corinth, and Alexandria, where he will have met other students from distant parts;[2] travel in those days was, for persons who could afford it, a common feature of higher education. At the age of twenty-eight Galen returned to his native Pergamum to practise medicine in connection with the local troupe of gladiators attached to the high priest of the Pergamene temples.[3] After about five years, in 162, he journeyed overland through Thrace and Macedonia to Rome, evidently along the same route which the ailing Aristides had taken just under twenty years before.[4] It was inevitable that at some point a man of superior education, wealth, and ambition would go to Rome, and it was there that Galen's fame began.

The peripatetic philosopher Eudemus introduced Galen to the consular Flavius Boëthus (himself a Syrian from Ptolemais),[5] and it was perhaps with the encouragement and patronage of Boëthus that Galen presented a series of public anatomical displays which attracted a number of well-known and important Romans. The displays seem to have been held over a period of three years and to have been very much to the taste of the people of that time.[6] In Galen's audience were L. Sergius Paullus, *consul ordinarius* for the second time in 168

---

[1] *Galeni in Platonis Timaeum Commentarii fragmenta*, ed. H. O. Schröder (1934), p. 99. The fragment from which these lines come concerns Galen's autopsy. Text and context refute Behr, op. cit., p. 162.

[2] Galen 2. 217; 19. 16 [97 Mueller] (Smyrna); 2. 217 ff., 660 (Corinth); 12. 177, 905, 13. 599, 15. 136 (Alexandria) Kühn. Cf. *PIR*[2], G 24.

[3] Galen 13. 599 ff., 18 B. 567 Kühn. On the gladiators attached to the ἀρχιερεύς, see L. Robert, *Les Gladiateurs dans l'orient grec* (1940), p. 285.

[4] Galen 2. 215; 8. 226, 361; 14. 605 Kühn (cf. *PIR*[2], G 24). For Aristides' journey, Aristid. 48. 60 Keil.

[5] Galen 14. 612 Kühn; *PIR*[2], F 229 (cf. G 24). The date of Boëthus' consulate is unknown.   [6] Galen 14. 626 ff. Kühn. Cf. *PIR*[2], G 24.

and prefect of the city, M. Vettulenus Civica Barbarus, *consul ordinarius* in 157 and uncle of Lucius Verus, and Cn. Claudius Severus, *consul ordinarius* for the second time in 173.[1] Galen also attracted sophists and rhetors like Hadrian of Tyre and Demetrius of Alexandria.[2] Connections between some of these consuls and sophists are independently shown in other sources. Such, for example, is the link between Claudius Severus and Hadrian of Tyre attested on a verse inscription from Ephesus.[3] Here as witnesses of skilful expositions of anatomy these men are found united by a common curiosity about the body and disease. When Flavius Boëthus went out to govern the province of Syria Palaestina, he solicited from Galen helpful writings to consult. Galen had cured Boëthus' wife and son in time past, and Boëthus would not be without his counsel in the future.[4] However, as Galen observes, Boëthus died in Syria.[5]

It was Cn. Claudius Severus who carried the fame of Galen to Marcus Aurelius. This occurred at some point during the season of anatomical displays, since Galen declares that Lucius Verus was away for the Parthian War.[6] With the penetration of the plague into Italy Galen himself left the country, only to be recalled, after Lucius' return, for the very reason of the plague.[7] Marcus and Lucius summoned him to Aquileia; and after Lucius' death Marcus begged Galen to remain with him in the Marcomannic campaign. But Galen was successful in securing permission to reside at Rome as physician to the prince Commodus, and he remained in Rome as court physician until his death in 199.[8] In those last thirty years Galen's prestige was at its height. He served, at one time or another, Commodus, Marcus, Septimius Severus, and the influential

---

[1] Galen 14. 629 Kühn. On L. Sergius Paullus, *PIR*, S 377. For M. Vettulenus Civica Barbarus, see R. Syme, *Athenaeum* 35 (1957), 306 ff. and below, p. 82. Note also a Βάρβαρος ὑπατικός at Pergamum (*Ath. Mitt.* 29 [1904], 162, l. 9). On Cn. Claudius Severus, *PIR²*, C 1024.
[2] Galen 14. 629 Kühn. For the identification of Demetrius with the Aelius Demetrius of *OGIS* 712, cf. C. P. Jones, *CQ* 17 (1967), 311 f.
[3] *PIR²*, C 1024 and *JÖAI* 40 (1953), 14.
[4] Galen 2. 215; 14. 641; 19. 15–16 Kühn (the last = 96 Mueller).
[5] Galen 19. 16 Kühn = 96 Mueller.
[6] Galen 14. 647 Kühn.
[7] Galen 14. 649 ff.; 19. 14 ff. and 17 ff. Kühn (94 ff. and 98 ff. Mueller).
[8] Galen 14. 650; 19. 18 Kühn (98–9 Mueller).

sophist Aelius Antipater, *ab epistulis* to Severus.[1] He continued to be in touch with men like Claudius Severus.[2] He appears as a leading participant in the discussion of Athenaeus' deipnosophists at the house of P. Livius Larensis, a minor pontifex.[3] In an utterance of justifiable pride Galen wrote that purely as a result of his professional accomplishments he had become known to the leading men at Rome and to all the emperors in succession.[4]

Not that doctors of the court had in the past gone unnoticed. But, as in so many aspects of the high empire, the pattern of the past now becomes more conspicuous and more important. Because of their merciful calling doctors had always been sought after by cities and kings alike, so that the development of the medical schools in the Hellenistic Age lies in many ways at the centre of the history of medicine in antiquity after Hippocrates. The so-called public doctors supplied from the school on Cos to distant parts of the Mediterranean world, the many epitaphs and epigrams—literary and epigraphical—of doctors all illustrate vividly the demand for their services throughout the Hellenistic and Roman eras.[5] The public and private doctors, the diverse role of the ἰατρὸς δημοσιευόντων of the Hellenistic period and the δημόσιος ἰατρός of the Roman belong to any account of ancient medicine or indeed to any account of social welfare in antiquity.[6] The need for healing was constant. But the career of Galen betokens an exaggerated popularity of medicine as such among the educated classes of East and West, and the popularity of medicine as a subject is by no means the same nor so constant as the need for it.

Many of the doctors of the Roman emperors can be named

---

[1] Galen 14. 651 ff. (Commodus); 14. 4 ff., 657 ff. (Marcus); 14. 65–6 (Severus); 14. 218 (Antipater) Kühn.

[2] Cf. Galen 14. 653, 654, 656 Kühn.

[3] Cf. W. Dittenberger, 'Athenäus und sein Werk', *Apophoreton* (1903), pp. 1 ff. On P. Livius Larensis, cf. *ILS* 2932.

[4] Galen 8. 144 Kühn: ἀπό τε τῶν ἔργων τῆς τέχνης ἐγνώσθην, οὐκ ἀπὸ λόγων σοφιστικῶν, τοῖς τ' ἄλλοις τῶν ἐν Ῥώμῃ πρώτων ἀνδρῶν καὶ πᾶσιν ἐφεξῆς τοῖς αὐτοκράτορσιν.

[5] See L. Robert, *Rev. de Philol.* 13 (1939), 163–73; *Hellenica* 2 (1946), 103 ff.; L. Cohn-Haft, *The Public Physicians of Ancient Greece* (1956), pp. 21–2. For papyri, *Eos* 48, i (1956), 181 ff.

[6] Cohn-Haft, op. cit., pp. 6–7. Note Th. Meyer, *Geschichte des römischen Arztestandes* (1952).

and contrasted with Galen. Several, appropriately, bear the name Asclepiades.[1] Asclepius was the god of healing, the patron deity of doctors, hence the term Asclepiad which occurs commonly (never to be confused with a different term, Asclepiast).[2] Certain of the early imperial physicians acquired considerable recognition and honour through their good service: such was Antonius Musa in the court of Augustus or C. Stertinius Xenophon in the court of Claudius. For saving his life in 23 B.C. Augustus granted the golden ring to Musa with various exemptions,[3] and to Xenophon Claudius granted that much and more. In the fashion of the great envoys and rhetors, Xenophon was able to secure the emperor's good will for his native island of Cos, while he himself advanced to the post of *ad responsa graeca* and acquired—it would appear—comfortable estates in the Hellenic area of Naples.[4] Precious inscriptions have filled out our knowledge of T. Statilius Crito, physician to the emperor Trajan.[5] With his origins in the town of Heraclea in the plateau of Tabae in Caria, Crito rose to be designated φίλος of the emperor and accompanied him on at least one of his campaigns in Dacia. Like Plutarch, he was appointed an imperial procurator,[6] and it is worth noticing that later, under Marcus and Lucius possibly, a descendant of Crito, Statilius Critonianus, turns up as *procurator Augusti* in Thrace.[7] Such superior doctors as Musa, Xenophon, and Crito received honour and favour from their emperors as a result of outstanding service, and their careers provide appropriate antecedents for that of Galen. But there is no indication that they

---

[1] e.g. M. Artorius Asclepiades (*PIR*[2], A 1183) or C. Calpurnius Asclepiades (*ILS* 7789). Cf. S. Reinach, Daremberg–Saglio s.v. médecine (1689–91, *médecins de cours*).

[2] Cf. Cohn-Haft, op. cit., p. 30 (on Asclepiads, i.e. physicians not necessarily connected with the cult of Asclepius; and on Asclepiasts, i.e. members of a cult of Asclepius but not necessarily physicians).

[3] Dio 53. 30. 3.   [4] *P–W* Zweite Reihe, 6. 2450.

[5] W. H. Buckler, 'T. Statilius Crito, Traiani Augusti medicus', *JÖAI* 30 (1937), Beibl. 5–8; cf. *SEG* 4. 521. Further on Crito: L. Robert, *Hellenica* 3 (1946), 8–9; *La Carie* ii (1954), p. 167, no. 49; pp. 178–9, no. 75; pp. 200–1, no. 126.

[6] See the citations in the foregoing note. L. Robert, *Hellenica*, loc. cit., points out that the name of Crito's city of origin, Ulpia Heraclea, may well reveal Crito's influence with the emperor Trajan in obtaining special consideration for Heraclea.   [7] *IGR* 4. 855.

were sought after by the educated public of the time for lectures on medical topics and handbooks on disease for the lay reader. There is no indication that the lay reader wanted such things.

Yet there certainly existed a taste for medicine in the second century. Galen was a lion of society. The explanation lies in the old nexus between philosophy, oratory, and medicine. Mention has already been made of the situation in the second half of the fifth century B.C. : it will be recalled that the spread of Hippocratic medicine and the sophistic movement coincided. Similarly the so-called Second Sophistic was accompanied by a wave of popular enthusiasm for medicine. The issue here is one of tastes and cultural developments, not of positive and lasting achievements; for it would be justifiable to maintain that in oratory, philosophy, and medicine far more real progress was made in other centuries than the second A.D. Yet the growing taste for these disciplines, so closely intertwined in antiquity, is unmistakable from the very period with which Philostratus began his account of the sophistic revival, that is—just after the middle of the first century A.D. The important inscription recording provisions for the immunity of teachers under Vespasian links the παιδευταί who were *grammatici* and rhetors, with the ἰατροί, and this is a significant conjunction that persists throughout the subsequent immunity legislation.[1] In the edict of Hadrian on this subject there occur rhetors, philosophers (whom he was the first to include), and doctors, while the same conjunction reappears in the restrictive edict on immunities issued by Antoninus Pius.[2] We happen to know that the Mouseia of the larger eastern cities included both professors and physicians.[3] Even the declamations of pseudo-Quintilian provide a parallel in the school-problem of whether an orator, philosopher, or doctor is most useful to a state.[4]

Philostratus, in the earlier part of the *Lives of the Sophists*, acknowledges the connection between philosophy and rhetoric

---

[1] R. Herzog, *Sitzungsberichte preuss. Akad.* (Phil.-Hist. Klasse), 1935, p. 968 = McCrum–Woodhead, *Documents of the Flavian Emperors* (1961), no. 458. See above, p. 32.
[2] *Dig.* 27. 1. 6. 2 and 8.   [3] Cf. Herzog, op. cit., p. 1006.
[4] Pseudo-Quintil., no. 268, pp. 92 ff. Ritter.

by discussing the careers of those philosophers whom he regards as sophists. He does not indicate so explicitly the link with medicine, but it emerges from various biographical details: a teacher of the sophist Polemo, Timocrates from Pontic Heraclea, had begun his education with the intention of becoming a doctor.[1] Aristides describes Galen's teacher, Satyrus, both as a doctor and as a sophist.[2] The existence of the professional titles ἰατροσοφιστής and ἰατροφιλόσοφος illustrates distinctly the bond between the three professions.[3] The best commentary for these titles (although neither is mentioned there) is the opening of Plutarch's dialogue on good health.[4] Moschion and Zeuxippus, the interlocutors, begin their discussion with remarks about a certain doctor, Glaucus, who is described as ill-disposed toward philosophy. Glaucus was a doctor who believed that philosophy and medicine were as remote from each other as they could possibly be. Very different was the opinion of the interlocutor Moschion, who was angered by any philosopher without an interest in medicine and affirmed the interrelation of the two disciplines.[5] The pugnacious independence of Glaucus is reminiscent of outbursts by the sophist Aristides against the tribes of philosophers.[6]

A striking example of an ἰατροφιλόσοφος can be discovered among the contemporaries of Plutarch: the Stoic philosopher and poet Serapion, to whom Plutarch dedicated his dialogue on the epsilon at Delphi.[7] Thanks to a monument at Athens Serapion has become better known than Plutarch makes him. To be sure, an interest in medicine can be inferred from the examples which Serapion adduces within the pages of Plutarch, but the Serapion monument preserves the text of a poem by him on the proper behaviour of a doctor when confronted by

---

[1] VS, p. 536. [2] Aristid. 49. 8 Keil.
[3] e.g., an ἰατροφιλόσοφος in Baillet, Inscriptions grecques et latines des tombeaux des rois ou syringes (1926), 1298; an ἰατροσοφιστής in Anth. Pal. xi. 281 (cf. Suid., s.v. Gesios). Dio Prus. 33. 6 seems to refer to demonstration lectures of iatrosophists; Dio may not actually designate them as such, although von Arnim suggests emending τῶν καλουμένων ἰατρῶν to τῶν καλουμένων ἰατροσοφιστῶν (or λογιάτρων).
[4] Plut. De tuenda sanitate 122 B ff.
[5] Ibid., 122 D: τῷ μὴ φιλιατροῦντι χαλεπαίνεις φιλοσόφῳ.
[6] Cf. Aristid. ii, pp. 399 ff. Dindorf, 'On the Four'.
[7] See J. H. Oliver, Hesperia, Suppl. 8 (1949), 243–6.

a beautiful female patient. This is the work known by the title
which Paul Maas gave to it, *carmen de officiis medici moralibus*.[1]
On the inscription at Athens, Serapion is explicitly designated poet and Stoic philosopher: the union of poetry and
philosophy is familiar, and so too is the union of poetry and
medicine (one may profitably observe Nicander of Colophon
or indeed Serapion's contemporary, Marcellus of Side).[2] Serapion is very much a product of his own times, which cherished
and encouraged the interaction of disciplines. His interest in
medicine is the most valuable new fact about him and makes
it perfectly natural that—as the same inscription reveals—his
grandson should have been a priest of Asclepius. Furthermore,
his great-grandson was Q. Statius Themistocles, the keybearer
of Asclepius who is proclaimed related to philosophers, Asiarchs,
and consuls.[3]

The foregoing account of the way in which the sophistic
revival of the late first and the second centuries is inextricably
bound up with the renaissance of other intellectual pursuits
should complement and confirm what is known of Galen's
extra-medical interests. As he tells us often enough himself, he
believed passionately in the connection between philosophy
and medicine, and he was indeed the author of a number of
purely philosophical commentaries on works by Plato, Aris-
totle, Theophrastus, and others.[4] His writings included general
treatises, for example, περὶ ἠθῶν and περὶ ὁμονοίας (this latter
a theme particularly beloved in the second century).[5] The
opinions of Galen on philosophy and medicine as comple-

---

[1] J. H. Oliver, loc. cit. For more on the connection of philosophy and medicine on inscriptions, see M. N. Tod, *JHS* 77 (1957), 138–9.

[2] Nicander: *Anth. Pal.* ix. 211 ff. Marcellus' ἰατρικά: Suidas, s.v. Marcellus
Sidetes (cf. Wilamowitz, 'Marcellus von Side', *Sitzungsberichte preuss. Akad.*
1928, pp. 3 ff.). See also P. De Lacy, 'Galen and the Greek Poets', *GRBS* 7
(1966), 259–66. On the *liber medicinalis* (in hexameters) of Q. Serenus, often
called Sammonicus, see below p. 107. For a conjunction of poetry, philosophy,
medicine, and also history, cf. the polymath honoured at Rhodiapolis in *IGR*
3. 733.

[3] Oliver, op. cit.

[4] Cf. G. Sarton, *Galen of Pergamum* (1954), pp. 25 ff. and Galen's *De libris
propriis* (in 19 Kühn and also in Mueller). Certain philosophical works survive
only in Arabic versions: there is a list of some of these in Sarton, op. cit.,
pp. 99–100.

[5] Galen 19. 45–6 Kühn = 121 Mueller.

mentary studies can best be seen in the brief essay on the subject 'The Best Doctor is also a Philosopher'.[1] It appears from the bibliography which Galen thoughtfully provided of his own writings that he also wrote on philological topics, such as the vocabulary of Cratinus, Eupolis, and Aristophanes, and more general works on verbal expression.[2] These subjects will not seem surprising when we reflect that among Galen's contemporaries were Pollux and Phrynichus. In so many points was Galen a representative figure of the cultural life of his epoch, an epoch that welcomed medicine, philosophy, and rhetoric all together and enthusiastically.

Medicine was above all the profession of Galen; and if the Second Sophistic movement signals among other things an intensified general interest in the human body and its diseases, so does another great renaissance of the same period: the renaissance of the cult of Asclepius. The cult had been in existence for many centuries, and temples to Asclepius in various parts of the empire were already of some antiquity.[3] But the god enjoyed a tremendous increase in popularity precisely during the sophistic revival, and this was not sheer coincidence. There had always been a close and noticeable association between Asclepius and the doctors, as the term Asclepiad shows. A great medical school at Cos flourished alongside a great Asclepieum, and similarly under the empire at Pergamum. For the god was a god of healing and therefore, appropriately, a patron deity of the healing art. And throughout the long coexistence of Asclepius and the medical profession there was never—as far as one can tell—any unseemly competition between the two.

There are indeed scholars who believe that in the imperial period, at least, positive collaboration can be detected between Asclepius and the doctors: 'the god learned medicine.'[4] If the

---

[1] Galen 1. Kühn = 1 ff. Mueller: On this, M. Isnardi, *Par. d. Pass.* 16 (1961), 257 ff. For an Arabic text of the work, see P. Bachmann, 'Galens Abhandlung darüber, dass der vorzügliche Arzt Philosoph sein muss', *NGA* 1965, no. 1.

[2] *De libris propriis*: 19. 8 ff. Kühn = 91 ff. Mueller. Cf. De Lacy, op. cit. (p. 68, n. 2 above).

[3] Cf. E. J. and L. Edelstein, *Asclepius* (1945).

[4] Ibid., vol. ii, ch. 3, 'Temple Medicine'.

god in his mysterious way prescribed, as he did, treatments for
the ailing who dreamt of him, there was no reason why his
treatments should not be medically acceptable. Sometimes
they were, but many times they were not: as a result of the
valuable compilation (now to hand) of testimonia on the
divine healings of Asclepius,[1] it is possible to survey conveniently a generous selection of examples. The student of
Aelius Aristides' autobiographical discourses will recall the
amazement of Pergamene doctors at some of the treatments
the god prescribed for him. For instance: 'When the harbour
waves were swollen by the south wind and ships were in dis-
tress, I had to sail across to the opposite side, eating honey and
acorns from an oak tree, and vomit; then complete purifica-
tion is achieved. All these things were done when the inflam-
mation was at its peak and had even spread right to the
navel.'[2] Contrast the sensible words of Galen: 'It has great
influence on the patient's doing all that is prescribed if he has
been firmly persuaded that a remarkable benefit to himself
will ensue.'[3] However reluctant modern man is to admit it,
there is no escaping the conclusion that the work of the doctors and of Asclepius was quite separate and that there was no
collusion.[4] Rational healing and spiritual (or psychological)
healing existed side by side; the doctors did not castigate the
prescriptions of the god or try to attract his patients. What we
find easy to forget is that he was *their* god. Thus, the second
century saw a simultaneous resurgence of both rational and
irrational healing.

The revival of Asclepius is best expressed in palpable form
by the construction of the great Asclepieum at Pergamum by
the consular Rufinus, the Ῥουφίνιον ἄλσος.[5] The reports of
Aristides furnish vivid pictures of the litterati and ex-consuls at
Pergamum for their health: cultivated conversations by day,
incubations by night. As the quotation from Aristides has
shown, however, life was not all comfort in the care of
Asclepius.

---

[1] Edelstein, op. cit., vol. i, Testimonia.   [2] Aristid. 47. 65 Keil.
[3] Galen 17 (2). 137 Kühn.
[4] This was the conclusion of Edelstein, op. cit., vol. ii, p. 173.
[5] See above, p. 61 with n. 1.

Another striking illustration of the new popularity of the god is the bizarre success of Alexander of Abonuteichus, the false prophet. The essay by Lucian on this strange figure of the second-century East is anything but sympathetic, but it is possible to recover a few facts about Alexander's career.[1] He founded an oracle of an invented snake-god named Glycon, which had an enormous vogue in the Graeco-Roman world.[2] Lucian alleges that the general Severianus credulously consulted the oracle before the disaster at Elegeia in 161, and we are told how Marcus Aurelius threw two live lions into the Danube at the bidding of Glycon.[3] Alexander's daughter married the ageing consular P. Mummius Sisenna Rutilianus (*consul suffectus* in 146),[4] and he was allowed to change the name of Abonuteichus to Ionopolis and to coin money with Glycon depicted on it.[5] Specimens of the Glycon coinage are in existence today.[6] The story of the popularity of Glycon belongs to the history of the Asclepius cult, because, as Lucian's essay makes quite clear, Alexander's serpent-god was simply a new version of the old serpent-god Asclepius. Glycon's genealogy is identical to that of Asclepius, and his very name suggests the sweetness and gentleness that were celebrated attributes of ἤπιος Ἀσκληπιός.[7] The existence of Glycon's oracle and his influence in high circles complement Aristides' account of the consulars at Pergamum.

The age of the Second Sophistic exhibited another characteristic that must have developed all too easily with the popularity of medicine and Asclepius. That is hypochondria, possibly the most disquieting aspect of Antonine society and inducing a sense of foreboding. It might seem odd enough that Galen's disquisitions on anatomy were attended by many of the most

---

[1] Lucian, *Alexander*: A. Stein, 'Zu Lukians Alexandros', *Strena Buliciana* (1924), pp. 257–65; A. D. Nock, 'Alexander of Abonuteichos', *CQ* 22 (1928), 160–2; M. Caster, *Études sur Alexandre ou le Faux-Prophète de Lucien* (1938).

[2] Lucian, *Alex.* 30.

[3] Ibid. 27 (Severianus), 48 (lions in the Danube).   [4] Ibid. 35.

[5] Ibid. 58. The modern name is still essentially Ionopolis: Inebolu (L. Robert, *Hellenica* 11/12 [1960], 62).

[6] See E. Babelon, 'Le Faux-Prophète, Alexandre d'Abonuteichos', *Rev. Num.* 4 (1900), 1–30. Lucian, *Alex.* 58, alludes to coins depicting Alexander himself on one side, but coins with his image are not known.

[7] On Glycon as a new Asclepius, cf. M. Caster, op. cit. (n. 1 above) pp. 35–6.

important people in Rome, much as they attended the declamations of Hadrian of Tyre, or that Aristides should have been able to maintain his influential contacts without leaving the precinct of Asclepius at Pergamum. Yet we have, besides, abundant and often disagreeable evidence for an inordinate obsession with bodily ailments which has to be denominated hypochondria. 'I am one of those', said Aristides, 'who think that sickness is advantageous and who have acquired precious gems in return for which I would not accept all that which is considered happiness among men.'[1] And Aristides took exceptional pleasure in recording all his symptoms as well as all the peculiar treatments which the god prescribed for them.

Aristides' hypochondria was of an advanced kind. But a similar preoccupation pervades the correspondence between Fronto and Marcus Aurelius. Here, for example is an exchange between the two: Fronto to Marcus: 'I am anxious to know, my Lord, how you are keeping. I have been seized with pain in the neck. Farewell, my Lord. Greet your Lady.'[2] Marcus replies: 'I think I have got through the night without fever. I have taken food without repugnance, and am doing very nicely now. We shall see what the night brings. But, my master, by your late anxiety you can certainly gauge my feelings when I learnt that you had been seized with pain in the neck. Farewell, my most delightful of masters. My mother greets you.'[3]

One of the most astonishing letters in the whole collection of Fronto's correspondence is this, worthy of Aristides: Marcus to Fronto: 'This is how I have passed the last few days. My sister was seized suddenly with such pain in the privy parts that it was dreadful to see her. Moreover, my mother, in the flurry of the moment, inadvertently ran her side against a corner of the wall, causing us as well as herself great pain by the accident. For myself, when I went to lie down I came upon a scorpion in my bed; however, I was in time to kill it before lying down upon it. If you are better, that is a consolation. My mother feels easier now. Farewell, best and sweetest of masters. My lady greets you.'[4] Letters of this kind are not rare

---

[1] Aristid. 23. 16 Keil.   [2] Fronto, *Epist.*, p. 75 van den Hout.
[3] Ibid., pp. 75–6 van den Hout.
[4] Ibid., pp. 74–5 van den Hout. Fronto translations by C. R. Haines.

in the Fronto collection,[1] and they are something quite new to epistolography. In all the vast correspondence of Cicero, Seneca, and Pliny there is nothing to compare with what appears in the letters of Marcus and Fronto. To be sure, Cicero sometimes complains of *lippitudo*, and Seneca can show himself neurotic on occasion. But many letters, often detailed, exclusively on matters of pain and illness are something else again. Aristides was more characteristic of his age than many admirers of it would like to think.

Nor are we confined to Aristides, Marcus, and Fronto for displays of hypochondria. A long Oxyrhynchus text, evidently written by a highly literate person and originating in the second century, contains such things as this: 'It was night, when every living creature was asleep except those in pain . . . ; a violent fever burned me, and I was convulsed with loss of breath and coughing, owing to the pain proceeding from my side.'[2] These are the words of a worshipper of Asclepius, like Aristides. In that unhappy night the speaker describes how Asclepius appeared to him—as he regularly did—in a dream; for hypochondriacs dreams are important.

Men of considerable intelligence in the second century attached great value to dreams, men like Galen's father (whose dream determined Galen's career),[3] Marcus Aurelius (who acknowledges the role of his dreams in a passage of the Meditations),[4] or Cassius Dio (to whose dreaming we owe the Roman History).[5] An inscription recorded a dream of the sophist Polemo at Pergamum.[6] And through an appropriate accident the one great dream book which has survived from antiquity is Artemidorus' *Oneirocritica*, which seems to belong to the

---

[1] Cf. Fronto, *Epist.*, pp. 73–87 van den Hout. The letters on health all belong, it appears, to Book V of the Epistles to Marcus before 161. The arrangement is by subject-matter, rather than by chronology. Mommsen's account (*Hermes* 8 [1874], 212 = *Ges. Schr.* 4. 483) of a chronological arrangement, whereby letters from 147–61 are all implausibly packed into Book V, has to be rejected. Book V also contains the *Empfehlungsbriefe*.

[2] *P. Oxy.* 1381, col. v.   [3] See above p. 60.

[4] Marcus Aurelius, *Ad se ipsum* 1. 17. 9.

[5] Dio 72. 23 (Boissevain, pp. 304–5). Cf. *Gnomon* 37 (1965), 470. One might also adduce Favorinus' dream (*VS*, p. 490), Hermocrates' dream (*VS*, p. 611), or, for that matter, Lucian's *Somnium*.

[6] Phrynichus, p. 494 Rutherford. Cf. the anecdote about Polemo in the Pergamene Asclepieum in *VS*, p. 535.

Antonine period.[1] It would be interesting, if not perhaps agreeable, to have for comparison with it an earlier work—for example one (which Artemidorus disliked) by Artemon of Miletus: twenty-two books on dreams fulfilled through the agency of Serapis.[2] A comparison with the Asclepius literature also suggests itself.[3]

Above all, Galen himself declared his belief in the efficacy of dreams: 'There are certain people who scorn dreams, omens, and portents. But I know that I have often made a diagnosis from dreams; and guided by two very clear dreams I once made an incision into the artery between the thumb and index finger of the right hand . . . I have saved many people by applying a cure prescribed in a dream.'[4] It is not surprising that the doctors dwelled in such harmony with their patron god.

The prestige of Galen in educated Graeco-Roman society of the second century was symptomatic. Galen was a particularly brilliant representative of his age—hence his preferment. In his own person he combined those intellectual talents which had come into fashion. He was a physician, but also a philosopher and a man who studied old vocabulary. His anatomical demonstrations would probably have qualified him for the title of iatrosophist. And he came from Pergamum, one of the great cities of Asclepius. The second century was an age of hypersensitivity in literature and bodily care;[5] the joint efflorescence of an Aristides, a Galen, and a Herodes Atticus was not accidental. By an explicable and almost inevitable evolution the Second Sophistic brought with it a tendency to hypochondria which seems to mirror the excessive refinements of its rhetoric. The Antonine world was on the whole a peaceful one;

---

[1] Available in the old edition of R. Hercher (1864) and the new one of R. Pack (1963).

[2] Artemidorus, *Oneirocritica* 2. 44 (p. 179 Pack).

[3] The comparison is made fully by C. A. Behr, *Aelius Aristides and the Sacred Tales* (1968), chap. VIII and Appendix D.

[4] Galen 16. 222 Kühn. Note the sane remark of A. C. Lloyd, *JRS* 56 (1966), 254: 'But if most doctors believed in dreams and many (including Galen) in amulets, the evidence is that the bulk of their treatment and their surgery was not irrational or in historical perspective unscientific.'

[5] E. R. Dodds sees an 'Age of Anxiety': *Pagan and Christian in an Age of Anxiety* (1965), pp. 45 ff.

the era was, as Gibbon observed, one of felicity, when there was perhaps the leisure for delicate and refined tastes to find their fullest expression. In the midst of that glorious era there *was* a real illness, but Galen could do nothing about it. Unknowingly, he too suffered from it.

VI

ROMAN FRIENDS

THE relations of sophists with their emperors have already provided a theme, an important one; and the imperial circle has provoked an examination of the relations between sophists and doctors in the second century, their fortunes being so closely linked together. The sophists' friends who were not emperors must now be evoked, examined, and catalogued. Relations with each other and certain common origins will emerge. Roman friends will, necessarily in studying that ecumenical world, include persons from all parts of it; there will be African Romans, Greek Romans, Asian Romans. Discussion has to be prosopographical. Not every ascertainable friend can be included, nor can those that are included always be satisfactorily identified. The object is to discover something of the sophists' social milieu, outside their own cities and the imperial court.[1]

Several vexatious problems turn on the name Julianus. At the end of the fourth Sacred Discourse Aristides alludes to a ἡγεμών of that name.[2] Because of the sophist's reverse chronology in the discourse this proconsul can be assigned to the earliest part of the ten-year illness, and hence a date in the region of 144.[3] Who is this Julianus? An Ephesian inscription, datable to 145, provides the end of the current proconsul's name: - - - lianus.[4] Scholars have seen in this the person Ti.

---

[1] The persons discussed in the text which follows are grouped together so that related problems may be presented in proximity.

[2] Aristid. 50. 107 Keil.

[3] Cf. above, pp. 36 ff. for the chronology of Aristides' illness. See also A. Boulanger, *Aelius Aristide* (1923), pp. 461 ff. and C. A. Behr, *Aelius Aristides and the Sacred Tales* (1968), pp. 56–7, n. 1 and p. 134.

[4] *SIG*³ 850, l. 19. The inscription, communicated to W. H. Waddington by J. T. Wood, was first published by Waddington (with acknowledgement) in his *Mémoire sur la chronologie de la vie du rhéteur Aelius Aristide* (1867), pp. 7–8. Waddington gives ΥΛΙΑΝΟΥ as the surviving letters of the proconsul's name. However, the text which Wood himself published shows only ΛΙΑΝΟΥ as

Claudius Julianus and have identified him with Aristides' pro-consul. The dates seem to fit, and the proconsulate is duly fixed in 145/6 (although 144/5 would be equally possible).[1] There-fore, this Julianus must have had a consulate about the year 130.[2] Now it happens that a brick-stamp survives with a date given as the consulate of Julianus and Castus; neither consul is otherwise attested.[3] As the result of a fundamental study, this consular pair can be located in 129 or 130.[4] Aristides and the inscription from Ephesus do not enter the argument. It is, therefore, agreeable to think that the consul Julianus of the brick-stamp is the subsequent Asian proconsul in Aristides, and furthermore that the epigraphically attested - - - lianus, if a Julianus, is also this man. Chronological indications cohere.

But there is trouble. Fragments of the Ostian *fasti* provide the names of Castus and Julianus in the same year.[5] The pre-cise date of these consuls cannot be determined: it has to fall in the reign of Marcus or perhaps of Pius.[6] A remarkable and disturbing coincidence, in view of the pair on the brick-stamp.

surviving: *Discoveries at Ephesus* (1877), Appendix: Inscriptions from the Odeum, p. 6, no. 3; and this is confirmed by the transcription in *Inscr. Brit. Mus.* 3. 2, no. 491. Therefore, Waddington's version is quite simply a mistake made in communication or publication. W. Hüttl, *Antoninus Pius* ii (1933), p. 46, affirmed that Waddington had actually read ΥΛΙΑΝΟΥ (Hüttl refers to *Fastes*, no. 138): ignorant of Waddington's *Mémoire*, Hüttl was ignorant of Wood's communication, to say nothing of Wood's publication. L. Petersen (*Klio* 48 [1967], 162–3) perpetuates Hüttl's mistake and wrongly reproaches Dittenberger: 'Dittenberger liest nur noch 'Ιου]λιανός, während früher 'Io]υλιανός sichtbar gewesen und damit die Ergänzung gesichert ist.' *PIR²*, I 76 gives only the false reading. Let it be stated once and for all that no more of the name than ΛΙΑΝΟΥ stands or ever stood on the present fragment.

    [1] Cf. *PIR²*, C 896 and I 76. The Julianus on Ephesian coins, however, in an ἐπί dating-formula (cf. references in *PIR²*) ought to be a local magistrate, not a proconsul. Note the Ephesian Claudius Julianus under Trajan (*OGIS* 480 *ad fin.*). On the rarity of proconsul's names on coins with ἐπί but without ἀνθυπάτου cf. S. Jameson. *JRS* 55 (1965), 57, n. 32.
    [2] For the interval of approximately fifteen years between consulate and Asian proconsulate, see R. Syme, *REA* 61 (1959), 310–11.
    [3] Cf. A. Degrassi, *I fasti consolari dell'Impero Romano* (1952), p. 38. Also *CP* 39 (1944), 254–5.
    [4] H. Bloch, *I bolli laterizi e la storia edilizia romana* (1939) 281–2, 329; cf. L. Petersen, *Klio* 48 (1967), 161–2.
    [5] A. Degrassi, *Inscriptiones Italiae* 13. 1 (1947), p. 211: The fragment con-serves a reference to d]*ivae Faustinae*. Castus and Julianus are separated on the fragment by two other names and may not have been consular colleagues.
    [6] Ibid.

It is another matter whether the Julianus, consul and proconsul, is really a Ti. Claudius Julianus. A master in prosopo-
graphy, Edmund Groag, described the identification as *sine
causa* and promised a discussion of his own (which we must
now probably abandon all hope of seeing).[1] A *consul suffectus* in
159 (or 158) bears the name Ti. Claudius Julianus, obviously
not the proconsul. This man belonged to a great Ephesian
family: nephew of Ti. Julius Aquila, consul in 110, and grandson of Ti. Julius Celsus Polemaeanus, consul in 92 and benefactor of Ephesus; his father, married to Aquila's sister, would
seem to be a Ti. Claudius Julianus attested at Ephesus in the
time of Trajan.[2] Presumably the consul of about 159 was born
in the second decade of the second century, in the first half of
it; this would be right for a parent flourishing under Trajan.
It is not particularly suitable for the parent as consul *c.* 130.
Further, on inscriptions, the consul of about 159 proudly
acknowledges his relation to the consuls Aquila (his uncle) and
Polemaeanus (his maternal grandfather), but there is not
a word about his father.[3] And there would be, if he had been
a consul. It looks as if the marriage of Julianus' father to
Aquila's sister was the real cause of Julianus' good fortune,
not the career of the father himself. We are thus, on several
counts, deprived of any known Ti. Claudius Julianus to be
restored reasonably in the Ephesian inscription of 145 and to
be credited with a consulate about 130.[4]

However, Ti. Claudius Julianus, *consul suffectus* in 159 (or
perhaps 158), himself belongs in this account of sophists'
friends. Different from the man in Aristides, he is probably the
friend of Herodes Atticus. Correspondence with a Julianus is
mentioned in Philostratus' biography of Herodes.[5] The social

---

[1] E. Groag, *PIR*², C 876: he promised a discussion under the proconsul
Julianus in *PIR*². That entry has now appeared (*PIR*², I 76), containing
nothing by Groag.

[2] *PIR*², C 902. The consular year depends on the date of *CIL* 16. 110, on
which see A. Stein, *Die Reichsbeamten von Dazien* (1944), pp. 32 ff.

[3] *AE* 1905. 121 (mentioning Celsus Polemaeanus); *Forschungen in Ephesos*
5. 1. no. 7 (mentioning Aquila).

[4] In *Klio* 48 (1967), 159, L. Petersen has proposed that the consul and proconsul are in fact the Julius Julianus who has recently emerged as legate of
Arabia in 125: cf. *Israel Exploration Journal* 12 (1962), 259.

[5] *VS*, p. 552. Cf. *PIR*², C 902.

connections of Julianus through his father's marriage might
well have brought him into touch with the older man, Herodes.
The correspondent Julianus has also been identified with the
Antonius Julianus known to Aulus Gellius—hardly so plausible
a candidate, coming from Spain and lacking a fine pedigree.[1]

About the consul of 159, it must be observed finally that he is
certainly the friend of Fronto, appearing in the letters precisely as Claudius Julianus.[2] One letter, from the early part of
Marcus' reign, alludes to this Julianus as in command of an
armed province, and indeed the consul of about 159 is attested
in lower Germany in 160.[3] He will have remained there at
least into the next year. Thus, if we confess ignorance about
the Asian proconsul, something worth while can at least be
said about Herodes' friend—that he was an Ephesian of rank,
with consular antecedents, consul himself, and a friend of
Cornelius Fronto.

Among the gentilicia evoked by the name Julianus, Salvius
is important. In the second Sacred Discourse Aristides records,
in a context of about the year 145, that he met at Pergamum,
among the distinguished patients, a Salvius ὁ νῦν ὕπατος.[4]
This revelation presents a difficulty. The Sacred Discourses
were certainly composed after the plague had broken out,[5]
and after that date the only Salvius known as consul before
Aristides' death early under Commodus is P. Salvius Julianus,
consul in 175. Hence, it is normally thought, Aristides was
composing his discourse in 175: ὁ νῦν ὕπατος.[6] But is it altogether credible that the consul of 175 was taking a cure at
Pergamum and introduced to Aristides in 145? It is not impossible that Aristides met an ailing adolescent, but one would
have to be persuaded. Perhaps Aristides' memory has misled
him, for we know him not to be a consistently precise and
accurate chronologist. Another P. Salvius Julianus, almost

---

[1] *PIR*[2], A 844. The identification with Herodes' friend appears in the Loeb
Philostratus, *VS*, by W. C. Wright (1921), p. 153, where the man in Gellius is
called Antoninus (*sic*) Julianus.
[2] Fronto, *Epist.*, pp. 168, 174, 175 van den Hout. The man evidently bore the
agnomen Naucellius.
[3] Fronto, *Epist.*, p. 168 van den Hout: *tu provinciam cum exercitu administrares.*
Cf. *ILS* 2907 (Bonn).
[4] Aristid. 48. 9 Keil.   [5] Aristid. 48. 38 Keil (νόσος λοιμώδης).
[6] Cf., e.g., A. Boulanger, *Aelius Aristide* (1923), p. 162.

certainly the celebrated jurist, was consul in 148; he ought to be the man whom Aristides met. He was of a suitable age and status to be found among the prominent patients in the Asclepieum. Aristides, writing in a year—namely 175—in which he knew a Salvius Julianus was consul was quite capable of adding ὁ νῦν ὕπατος to the person of the same name whom he had met thirty years before.

It is difficult to know whether one ought in this context to try to exploit the opening of the Augustan History's life of Didius Julianus, where it is said that the jurist was twice consul and prefect of the city.[1] There is nothing absolutely against this. The life of the jurist can be traced as far as a proconsulate of Africa in 168/9.[2] In the period from 165 (and throughout the 170s) the consular fasti are lamentably incomplete, in many cases containing little more than the *ordinarii*. It might be possible to fit in the jurist with a second consulate: but a *consul bis* as a suffect would, in this period, be surprising. It is just possible that the *consul ordinarius* of 175 is none other than the jurist himself. The assumption that the Augustan History is right about his second consulate would have the merit of making sense of Aristides' remark. On the occasion of a second consulate one would expect him to be *ordinarius* again—especially if it is also to be believed that he became city prefect (an office almost always held in this period by men who held two consulates, the second as ordinarius).[3]

It has already emerged that the friends of M. Cornelius Fronto included Herodes' correspondent Ti. Claudius Julianus, *consul suffectus* in about 159.[4] The African rhetor had other

---

[1] *HA* Didius Julianus 1. 1.
[2] *ILS* 8973 (Pupput); *ILT* 799 (Thuburbo Maius). Cf. B. E. Thomasson, *Die Statthalter der römischen Provinzen Nordafrikas von Augustus bis Diokletianus* (1960), ii. 82–4.
[3] Note the following prefects of the city: L. Catilius Severus (*cos.* II *ord.* 120), M. Annius Verus (*cos.* II *ord.* 121, III *ord.* 126), M. Lollius Paulinus D. Valerius Asiaticus Saturninus (*cos.* II *ord.* 125), Sex. Erucius Clarus (*cos.* II *ord.* 146), Q. Junius Rusticus (*cos.* II *ord.* 162), L. Sergius Paullus (*cos.* II *ord.* 168), C. Aufidius Victorinus (*cos.* II *ord.* 183), P. (?) Seius Fuscianus (*cos.* II *ord.* 188). Only two known prefects of the city in this period did not have a second consulate: Ser. Scipio Salvidienus Orfitus, who was *cos. ord.* 110 and prefect *c.* 138 (perhaps dragged out by Hadrian at the end: Orfitus asked to be retired); and Q. Lollius Urbicus, *cos.* by 138 (year unknown), who may simply have died.
[4] See p. 79, above.

eastern contacts, as can be inferred from the preparations he had made for the Asian proconsulate which he never took up: *quo facilius a me tanta negotia per amicorum copias obirentur.*[1] One especially interesting case, which has only come to light in recent years, is L. Gavius Clarus, from a new senatorial family at Attaleia.[2] Between Fronto and Gavius there was a *vetus familiaritas*, of which Fronto saw fit to remind Lucius Verus, then in the East, when an impoverished Gavius was making his way to Syria to collect a legacy.[3]

Of the sophists, Favorinus and Herodes himself can be named as friends of Fronto. Favorinus is named only once in the letters, and that rather incidentally; but thanks to the *Attic Nights* of Aulus Gellius it is easy to discern the relationship with Fronto as well as to observe those trifling matters of archaic vocabulary and usage that were of supreme interest to both men.[4] Fronto's relations with Favorinus may have something to do with the curiously unfavourable opinion of Hadrian expressed in the correspondence (*fiducia mihi defuit*);[5] this, to be sure, depends on the view that Favorinus was exiled by Hadrian.[6] As for Herodes, the Fronto letters give ample evidence. In the beginning of their contact Fronto and Herodes were on opposite sides—in court; but a word from Marcus indicating his regard for the sophist led to a cordial *entente* between the two men.[7] It should be said, however, that many years later Fronto observed with evident pleasure that he was a great friend of Herodes, even though a speech in which he had denounced him was still in circulation.[8] The exact chronology of the trials and vicissitudes of Herodes in the face of hostility at Athens is not an easy matter, and it belongs rather to the topic of professional quarrels.[9]

[1] Fronto, *Epist.*, p. 161 van den Hout.
[2] *Türk Tarih Kurumu Belleten* 11 (1947), 101–4, nos. 19–20, and 22 (1958) 36–7, nos. 26–7 (whence *SEG* 17 [1960], nos. 584–5). Cf. *REG* 61 (1948), 201–2, no. 229, and 72 (1959), 255, no. 447.
[3] Fronto, *Epist.*, pp. 127–8 van den Hout.
[4] Fronto, *Epist.*, p. 204 van den Hout; Aul. Gell. *NA* 2. 26.
[5] Fronto, *Epist.*, p. 24 van den Hout.
[6] See above, pp. 36, 51–2.
[7] Fronto, *Epist.*, pp. 36–8 van den Hout.
[8] Fronto, *Epist.*, pp. 106 and 130 van den Hout.
[9] See below pp. 93–100.

Another of Herodes' friends was a certain Barbarus. All
modern editions of Philostratus have conspired to keep this
fact from scholars. Barbarus turns up twice in the *Lives of the
Sophists*, both times as an intimate of Herodes and once
qualified as ὕπατος (which is Philostratus' way of saying ὑπατικός).[1] In Kayser's edition and in the Loeb both appearances of
Barbarus have been removed and a Varus has replaced him
(Βᾶρος for Βάρβαρος).[2] But in 1937 an inscription was found in
the agora at Athens: it recorded the erection of a statue by
Herodes, the honorand being Κείβικα Βάρβαρον ὕπατον.[3] The
manuscripts of Philostratus were thus vindicated, and Civica
Barbarus made his début as a friend of Herodes. He was an
important person, uncle of Lucius Verus and consul in 157.[4]
A recent inscription from Argos reveals his full and correct
nomenclature, necessitating changes in most prosopographical
reference works. He is M. Vettulenus Sex. f. Civica Barbarus.[5]

Furthermore, Barbarus' sophistic contacts included the doctor Galen. At those exhibitions of anatomy between 162 and
165, Barbarus was regularly present.[6] It may be appropriate
next to turn to a consideration of a few other eminent Romans
who attended Galen's lectures. For the group is in itself a good
illustration of what sort of Romans were on terms with the
sophists. It will not be forgotten that in Galen's audience there
were Demetrius of Alexandria, Hadrian of Tyre, and others.[7]

One devotee of anatomy, L. Sergius Paullus, was consul for
the second time and *ordinarius* in 168, consul first in an unknown
year but—it would appear—before 162 (when Galen arrived

---

[1] *VS*, pp. 537 and 539. On p. 539 ὕπατος appears; for its meaning in Philostratus see above, p. 7, n. 1.
[2] Neither Kayser (in his Teubner text) nor Wright (in the Loeb) signal this
alteration anywhere, even though Kayser gives an apparatus (of sorts). The
manuscript readings can, however, be seen in Kayser's *editio maior* of Philostratus (1853), pp. 230 and 231. Editors, try as they will, cannot hide the truth
for ever: notice that in a new text of Pliny's letters the editor still prefers—in
spite of abundant evidence and a divided manuscript tradition—to name the
princeps Ephesiorum of Plin. *Ep.* 6. 31. 3 Ti. Claudius Ariston (*sic*). Cf. *Phoenix*
18 (1964), 327.
[3] *Hesperia* 7 (1938), 328: no text published but at least a decipherable
photograph, whence *AE* 1939. 109 (an imperfect text). The excavators finally
published the text in *Hesperia* 26 (1957), 220, no. 78.
[4] See R. Syme, *Athenaeum* 35 (1957), 306 ff.   [5] *AE* 1958. 15.
[6] Galen 14. 629 Kühn.   [7] Ibid.

in Rome).[1] He served as prefect of the city perhaps in the late sixties; he was, one supposes, a man of some consequence. But the evidence is thin and poor. Bishop Melito of Sardis, as quoted by Eusebius, mentions a proconsul of Asia by the name of Servilius Paullus in this period, and emendation has produced L. Sergius Paullus, proconsul of Asia under Marcus and Verus.[2] This is quite possible, but residual doubt must always remain. The name Servilius Paullus is not intolerable. There was, for instance, a legate to the emperor Hadrian from Alexandria Troas by the name of M. Servilius Tutilius Paullus.[3] And it is well known that ambassadors from a provincial city are drawn from the aristocratic cream of the place, and that the descendants of ambassadors often enough turn up in the senate at Rome.

Another friend of Galen was Cn. Claudius Severus, also a consul twice (*ordinarius* of the year 173) and perhaps prefect of the city.[4] The origins of this Severus are eastern, from Pompeiopolis in Paphlagonia. His father, Cn. Claudius Severus Arabianus, had been *consul ordinarius* in 146, and his grandfather had been suffect consul in 112.[5] The consul of 173 appears in the group of Galen and, it may be proposed, is a distinguishable friend of Fronto.[6] He is the recipient of a dedicatory epigram by the sophist Hadrian of Tyre. This important text declares that Hadrian has set up a statue to Severus the consular, described as father of an Ummidius Quadratus and a relative of emperors. The sophist identifies himself by the words Μούσαισι μέλων, and the relative of emperors is a man we know to have married (in a second union) a daughter of Marcus Aurelius.[7]

How was Cn. Claudius Severus the father of an Ummidius Quadratus? This is not clear; there was presumably an adoption by the consul of 167, M. Ummidius Quadratus, himself

---

[1] *PIR*, S 377. Galen did not reach Rome before 162: *PIR²*, G 24.

[2] Eusebius, *Hist. Eccl.* 4. 26. Cf. *PIR*, S 377 and A. Birley, *Marcus Aurelius* (1966), p. 328.

[3] *CIL* 3. 7282.   [4] See Appendix III below.

[5] *PIR²*, C 1024.

[6] For the connection with Galen, see above p. 63. On Fronto, Appendix III below.

[7] On all this, E. Groag, *Wiener Studien* 24 (1902), 261 ff. (whence *PIR²*, C 1024) is fundamental. The text is republished in *JÖAI* 40 (1953), 14.

son of a sister of Marcus Aurelius, namely Annia Cornificia, and grandson of the *consul suffectus* of 118.[1] In any case, the closeness of both Claudius Severus and the Ummidii Quadrati to the house of Marcus could not be clearer. One recalls that it was Severus who introduced Galen to Marcus and that it was Severus who made a not wholly favourable estimate of Hadrian the sophist's style[2]—which confirms some kind of association between the two men, though it need not suggest a falling out. Finally, there was Ummidius Quadratus, the young conspirator against Commodus.[3]

In connection with the persons whom Galen mentions, it may be as well to subjoin here the name of Arria, for what it may suggest of other contacts. Galen affirms that he cured this lady, a dear friend of his.[4] It has been suggested that Arria was the woman of that name known as the wife of M. Nonius Macrinus, consul in 154.[5] This is not a bad idea.

The preceding account of a puzzling Ummidius Quadratus calls up the many problems surrounding the name Quadratus in studies of the Second Sophistic. No answer can be given here: some of the important evidence may, however, be reviewed with profit in the interest of more general observations. First: Aristides' Quadratus, ὁ ἡμέτερος ἑταῖρος, a rhetor, and proconsul of Asia more or less (οἶμαι) in succession to Severus.[6] Philostratus mentions as teacher of Varus of Perge a Κοδρατίων ὁ ὕπατος, a sophist in the style of Favorinus.[7] It has customarily been supposed that Aristides' friend and Varus' teacher are the same, a consular rhetor and—it would be natural—of eastern origin. Possibly Pergamene, of the great family of Julii Quadrati; or better, he is L. Statius Quadratus, consul in 142 and an Athenian.[8] This candidate emerges from

---

[1] On this man (and other Ummidii of the age), cf. R. Syme, *Historia* 17 (1968), 72 ff. Also J. Fitz, *Epigraphica* 26 (1964), 45 ff.

[2] *VS*, p. 588: Σεβήρου δὲ ἀνδρὸς ὑπάτου διαβάλλοντος αὐτόν . . .

[3] See above, p. 55, and R. Syme, *Historia* 17 (1968), 72 ff.

[4] Galen 14. 218–19 Kühn.

[5] A proposal of Groag in *PIR²*, A 1116.

[6] Aristid. 50. 63 and 71 Keil. Therefore, the year will be *c.* 154.

[7] *VS*, p. 576, τὸν Φαβωρίνου τρόπον σοφιστεύων.

[8] On the Pergamene Julii Quadrati, see above p. 25. For L. Statius Quadratus and his provenance (denied without cause in *PIR*, S 640), see E. Groag, *Die römischen Reichsbeamten von Achaia von Augustus bis auf Diokletian* (1939), p. 171.

a vexing text in the *Martyrium Polycarpi* where a Statius Quadratus is named as proconsul at the time of Polycarp's martyrdom, and also from a straightforward but undated inscription
giving a L. Statius Quadratus as proconsul of Asia.[1] The dating
of Polycarp's martyrdom oscillates between a year under Pius
(probably 155) and under the *divi fratres* (perhaps in the late
sixties).[2] The evidence of Aristides points toward the earlier
option.[3] This notorious chronological problem does not seem
susceptible of resolution on present evidence, but manifestly it
cannot be suppressed in alluding to Aristides' friends.

Some scholars have canvassed an entirely fresh possibility
about the mysterious Quadratus. In view of the eastern connections of the Ummidius Quadratus in the Hadrian epigram
to Severus, perhaps the father of the consul of 167 is the proconsul and rhetor in Aristides. He could be assigned a consulate
in 140 or so.[4] But this is a rather less satisfactory Quadratus
than a man certainly eastern like L. Statius Quadratus.

From Syria came the intellectual men, Avidius Heliodorus
and Avidius Cassius, father and son. Heliodorus, it has already
been argued, was both philosopher and rhetor, rising to a prefecture of Egypt at the end of Hadrian's reign and serving in
that post for the first years of Pius.[5] Heliodorus was another
friend of Aristides, as is evident from the warm letters of support sent at the time of the immunity crises;[6] and it is more
than likely that Aristides' relations with Heliodorus can be
traced to his visit in Egypt precisely during the period when
Heliodorus is known to have been prefect there.[7] As for

On the proconsulate W. Hüttl, *Antoninus Pius* ii (1933), pp. 52 ff. However the
consul of 142 is not easy to accept as proconsul in *c*. 154/5 because the interval
between consulate and proconsulate is too short: R. Syme, *REA* 61 (1959), 311.

[1] Migne, *PG* 5. 1044–65; *IGR* 4. 1339 (Magnesia ad Sipylum).
[2] Cf. H. Grégoire, *Anal. Boll.* 69 (1951), 1 ff. (with *REG* 65 [1952], p. 174,
no. 145); H. Marrou, *Anal. Boll.* 71 (1953), 5 ff.; W. H. C. Frend, *Oikoumene*
(in honour of the Second Ecumenical Council), pp. 499–506. Eusebius, *Hist.
Eccl.* 4. 15. 1 clearly dates Polycarp's martyrdom to the *divi fratres*; similarly the
chronicle, under 166 in Latin (Helm) and 169 in Armenian (Karst).
[3] See now T. D. Barnes, *JTS* 18 (1967), 433 ff. and 19 (1968), 510 ff.
[4] So Groag, *Wiener Studien* 24 (1902), 264, and R. Syme, *JRS* 43 (1953),
152 and 159.
[5] *PIR*², A 1405; A. Stein, *Die Präfekten von Aegypten* (1950), pp. 72–4. Cf.
above, pp. 50–1. [6] Aristid. 50. 75 Keil.
[7] On Aristides' visit to Egypt, see *VS*, p. 582 and Aristid. 36 Keil (the

Heliodorus' rebel son, Avidius Cassius, a friend or at least a correspondent of Fronto, we have in Philostratus the famous letter of Herodes to Cassius in 175: ‛Ηρώδης Κασσίῳ· ἐμάνης.[1] In intellectual, philhellenic court circles, these two will undoubtedly have had many associates in common besides Fronto.

Another friend of Aristides, L. Cuspius Pactumeius Rufinus, appears several times in the fourth Sacred Discourse.[2] A Pergamene and a consul, he held office in the year 142 together with the Athenian L. Statius Quadratus.[3] There has been occasion before to discuss his magnificent contribution to the revival of the Asclepius cult at Pergamum, namely the ‛Ρουφίνιον ἄλσος.[4] Rufinus was known to Galen during his student years, when Galen and Aristides met. Aristides depended substantially on Rufinus' advice and intercession, and it would appear that Rufinus was often in residence at Pergamum in the late forties and early fifties during the construction of the Asclepieum.[5]

In three passages of the Sacred Discourses Aristides mentions his friendship at Pergamum with a certain Σηδᾶτος. The following facts emerge: Sedatus was a Roman senator of praetorian rank, his origin was Nicaea, and he was on terms with Rufinus in the Asclepieum.[6] Hence another eastern senator as friend of a sophist. Who is Sedatus? The name as a cognomen is not uncommon; however, no senatorial Sedatus can be tracked down in the second century. We are, of course, short of many names, but two details about Aristides' friend prompt speculation and emendation: he was in Pergamum in the late forties or very early fifties, and his rank then was praetorian. What is required is Σηδάτιος to replace Σηδᾶτος. The

---

Aegyptios). Also A. Boulanger, *Aelius Aristide* (1923), pp. 120–4, 489–90. With a birth-date in 117 (cf. above, p. 61, n. 3), Aristides' visit to Egypt will fall within Heliodorus' prefecture there. On Aristides' meeting with Heliodorus, see also D. Magie, *Roman Rule in Asia Minor* (1950), ii. 1492.

[1] *VS*, p. 563.
[2] Aristid. 50. 28, 43, 83, 84, 107 Keil.
[3] For the origin of Quadratus, see above, p. 84, n. 8.
[4] *Anth. Pal.* 9. 656. Cf. above, p. 61.
[5] Rufinus and Galen: 2. 224 Kühn (as emended, cf. p. 60, n. 8 above). For the date of the connections with Aristides at Pergamum, see above, p. 39.
[6] Aristid. 48. 48 Keil (a senator), 50. 16 Keil (from Nicaea and praetorian), 50. 43 Keil (Rufinus).

man will be M. Sedatius Severianus, *consul suffectus* in 153 and therefore ideally suited to be found with praetorian rank in the latter period of Aristides' illness.[1] There is reason to think that he might have incubated in the Asclepieum: Lucian tells that Severianus consulted Glycon, the serpent-god of the false prophet Alexander, in 161, before he set out for the disaster at Elegeia.[2] Since Glycon functioned as a νέος Ἀσκληπιός,[3] it would not surprise to find Sedatius Severianus earlier in the care of Asclepius himself.

Lucian describes Severianus as a 'foolish Celt'.[4] Hence the common view that he came from Germany. But there were also Celts in Asia Minor, where the language went on being spoken into the fifth century.[5] Lucian means by Κελτός simply one of those foreigners who dwelt in Asia Minor. Derogatory national epithets, not necessarily very accurate, were conventional ingredients of ancient abuse.[6] Lucian's hostile designation of Severianus need not prohibit the identification with Aristides' friend.

Several times in the history of the Second Sophistic there appears the brothers Quintilii. This remarkable pair turns up in some capacity in Achaea, either as proconsul and legate (the conventional view) or as *corrector* and *comes*; they were on bad terms with Herodes.[7] They appear next in Asia. Marcus visited Smyrna in 176 and asked to meet Aristides; the Quintilii duly located the sophist and presented him to the emperor.[8] The brothers had been consuls together in 151: what they were doing in Asia in 176 is by no means clear. One of them ought to have been a proconsul, but the interval from the consulate is too long.[9] They appear next on the Danube in 178.[10]

[1] This suggestion was made (without, however, any reference to Lucian) by B. Borghesi, *Œuvres complètes* (1872), viii. 473, and endorsed by Mommsen, *ad CIL* 3. 1575.   [2] Lucian, *Alex.* 27.

[3] Ibid. 14. Also M. Caster, *Études sur Alexandre ou le Faux-Prophète de Lucien* (1938), pp. 35–6.   [4] Lucian, *Alex.* 27.

[5] Jerome, *PL*, vol. 26 Migne (Hieron., vol. 7), col. 430.

[6] Cf. W. Süss, *Ethos* (1910), pp. 247 ff., and R. G. M. Nisbet, *Commentary on Cicero's In Pisonem* (1961), p. 194. Cf. Julian against the Christians, κατὰ Γαλιλαίων.   [7] *VS*, p. 559.   [8] *VS*, p. 582.

[9] On the interval, see above p. 84, note 8. Observe also *Dig.* 38. 2. 16. 3, a rescript from the *divi fratres* to the *Quintilii fratres* (? in Asia).

[10] Dio 71. 33. 1. E. Groag argued that Dio is here referring to the famous brothers (both *cos.* 151), rather than to their sons (one *cos.* in 172, the other in

The Quintilii came from Alexandria Troas: Herodes alluded to this in a jest at their expense.[1] Their father and their grandfather had both been senators and served in the East.[2] The Quintilii stand revealed as members of one of the great families of the Greek East in the second century, of an eminence to associate as equals with a Herodes or an Aristides. Commodus extinguished them, and in recording their deaths Cassius Dio observed that they had a great reputation for culture, leadership, unanimity, and wealth—an irresistible combination of virtues.[3]

Through the accidents by which evidence survives, we have been left with an unbalanced supply of testimony on the Roman friends of sophists. This means that we are better off in discerning men known to Herodes or Aristides. (On Aristides there would be little indeed if one were confined to Philostratus' biography.) But even with this erratic distribution of evidence, two characteristics of the friendships or associations are striking: most of the 'Roman' friends were of eastern provenance, and most had numerous sophistic contacts. Things had progressed a long way from the old system of the close dependence of an eastern rhetor on some one important Roman aristocrat of the west. It is characteristic of the age that Roman intimates of sophists in the second century were largely cultivated men from their own part of the empire and, furthermore, tended to form an intellectual community within the empire. As pupils often passed from one sophist to another, so did friends. Within the frame of the Roman empire, men of Hellenic culture regularly adhered to each other, now that so many easterners themselves could be numbered among the Roman aristocrats.

180); *Die römischen Reichsbeamten von Achaia von Augustus bis auf Diokletian* (1939), p. 130, n. 544. Against this, and in favour of the sons: W. Reidinger, *Die Statthalter des ungeteilten Pannonien und Oberpannoniens* (1956), p. 88.

[1] *VS*, p. 559. Herodes said that he blamed Homer's Zeus for loving the Trojans.

[2] Grandfather: *ILS* 1018, perhaps the recipient of Pliny, *Ep.* 8. 24, although the identification has been questioned by A. N. Sherwin-White, *The Letters of Pliny* (1966), p. 479. Father: *CIL* 14. 2609.

[3] Dio 72. 5. 3: μεγάλην γὰρ εἶχον δόξαν ἐπὶ παιδείᾳ καὶ ἐπὶ στρατηγίᾳ καὶ ὁμοφροσύνῃ καὶ πλούτῳ.

VII

PROFESSIONAL QUARRELS

So far the relations of sophists with the imperial court and the Roman aristocracy. Earlier an effort was made to define their role in the greater eastern cities. Now the relations, or rather bad relations, of sophists with one another must be examined. As often, it is in the friction of historical personalities that matters of interest are to be found. Some of the sophists' disputes do not, it can be readily granted, have any great importance; but they augment our available knowledge of life in eastern cities. Demonstrations staged for this teacher or that by crowds of partisan students make a bit more brilliant the picture of local affairs under the high empire. And at times, the quarrels of sophists did actually impinge on the great men of the day: attacks on Herodes Atticus became more than petty disturbances. Further, a polemical literature came into being in the form of tracts by warring sophists, denouncing each other with wit and erudition. Throughout all the accounts of sophistic animosity there is a strongly academic odour. One recognizes that exquisite polemic which arises so naturally in communities of the highly educated.

Philostratus found it necessary to comment specifically on the agreeable personality of Rufus of Perinthus. Despite Rufus' great reputation in Greece, Asia Minor, and Italy, he nowhere made any enemies; in fact he made benevolence his business.[1] Rufus' lack of enemies was exceptional. Philostratus produces certain instances of ill will that suggest there is more than he tells: such was the nastiness between Hermogenes and Antiochus or between Pollux and Athenodorus.[2] In the case of Proclus we are told that his feud was not merely with the Thessalian

[1] *VS*, p. 598: πρᾳότητος ἦν χρηματιστής.
[2] *VS*, p. 577: Antiochus cruelly observed that Hermogenes, the youthful prodigy, had grown up into a puerile adult. *VS*, pp. 594–5: Athenodorus mocked the childishness of Pollux.

sophist Hippodromus but that he inveighed against everyone who taught at Athens.[1] We know that the rivalry between Apollonius of Naucratis and Heracleides of Lycia erupted in the dismissal of Heracleides from his professorship at Athens: according to Philostratus Apollonius and his followers were able to accomplish this with the particular help of one Marcianus of Doliche.[2] At the very time at which Apollonius of Naucratis and Heracleides were teaching at Athens, so too was Apollonius of Athens; and this other Apollonius also exerted himself against the unfortunate Heracleides, who was publicly disgraced in a competition of declamation before the emperor Septimius Severus.[3] Heracleides is said to have been stripped of his immunity in consequence of his defeat by the Athenian Apollonius.[4] Professional squabbles could thus lead to such disagreeable outcomes as loss of job or privilege.

The troubles of some of the more famous sophists are occasionally better documented. (Not always, of course. One could recall the vexing passage in Cassius Dio in which Hadrian is credited with the overthrow of Favorinus and Dionysius by the wilful elevation of their antagonists.[5] There is nothing to be gained from further speculation on that passage.) We may consider the account in Philostratus of Favorinus' rivalry with Polemo. Those two titans of culture had special ties with eastern sophistic centres; Favorinus was the hero of Ephesus, Polemo of Smyrna. Neither was born in the city that cherished him, but of course neither was born in a sophistic centre.[6] The contest between Favorinus and Polemo was, therefore, the cultural contest between Ephesus and Smyrna. Rivalry for pre-eminence among the greater cities of Asia Minor was a common thing in this age, as even a cursory reading of Dio Chrysostom will show. Empty titles and imagined superiority meant much to the local citizenry. Accordingly, a great feud such as that between Favorinus and Polemo might easily be a manifestation of city rivalry. Sophists were cause for boasting, as were buildings, canals, or coinage.

[1] *VS*, p. 617.   [2] *VS*, p. 613.   [3] *VS*, p. 601.   [4] Ibid.
[5] Dio 69. 3. 4. Cf. above, pp. 52–3.
[6] *VS*, pp. 490–1. Favorinus was born in Arelate, Polemo in Laodicea on the Lycus.

Philostratus says that the quarrel of Favorinus and Polemo began in Ionia, but the two great men perpetuated it in Rome[1]—a source of delectation for upper-class Romans. Neither sophist could have had the slightest doubt but that the quarrel increased the reputations of both. It was certainly as profitable as Rufus' benevolent disposition. At Rome, observed Philostratus, consulars and sons of consulars applauded one sophist and then the other, starting 'a rivalry such as kindles the keenest envy and malice even in the hearts of wise men'.[2]

Another great quarrel of which we have some record involved the philosophic teacher of Polemo, Timocrates from Pontic Heraclea. The sophist Scopelian had taken to having himself depilated,[3] a preoccupation that was well suited to be a theme for invective. Timocrates attacked Scopelian, and— we are told—all the youth of Smyrna took sides in the conflict.[4] Polemo joined the faction of Timocrates, οἱ τοῦ Τιμο-κράτους στασιῶται.[5] Philostratus' language is redolent of civil war. That because there was none. In an era from which real struggles had vanished, these play-wars absorbed local emotions. When Timocrates and Scopelian had gone to their graves, the στασιῶται, probably under the strong leadership of Polemo, reached an *entente* in order to make war on Ephesus and Favorinus.

Hadrian of Tyre figured in a lively dispute at Athens, where he was professor of rhetoric. Hadrian's antagonist was Chrestus of Byzantium, who happened to have a devoted disciple of unpleasant habits. (Philostratus claims that the man used to bark insults.[6]) Hadrian was prepared to tolerate the vile abuse of Chrestus' disciple, but Hadrian's own assembled disciples were not. The faithful pupils of Hadrian had the barking man thrashed, causing his intestines to swell. After thirty days of heavy drinking, the man died; and Hadrian

---

[1] *VS*, p. 490. It is possible that the sophist whom Hadrian promoted when he wanted to overthrow Favorinus (cf. Dio 69. 3. 4) was none other than Polemo. On the possibility of Hadrian's having exiled Favorinus, see above p. 36. Note Polemo's vicious description of a man who can be none other than Favorinus in *Physiog.*, pp. 161–5 (vol. i Foerster).

[2] *VS*, p. 490. [3] *VS*, p. 536. [4] Ibid.

[5] Ibid. Polemo was a pupil of both men.

[6] *VS*, p. 587: ὑλάκτει.

was accused of murder before the proconsul.[1] A vociferous crowd of Greeks spoke up for the sophist and wept, while a doctor—doubtless a public one—gave testimony on the alcoholism of the deceased.[2] Presumably Hadrian was acquitted. But Chrestus commanded a large Athenian following too. We have it that when Hadrian was translated to the chair at Rome an embassy was on the point of going out from Athens to ask the emperor to appoint Chrestus. It was Chrestus himself who put a stop to that.[3] Once again the enthusiasms of a city can be seen through the fortunes of sophists.

The quarrel between Aspasius of Ravenna and Philostratus of Lemnos followed the reverse development of that between Favorinus and Polemo. This later quarrel began in Rome, where Aspasius was professor, and it grew more serious in Ionia.[4] Other sophists took sides; one of these was a certain Cassianus with one famous pupil, who was a Lydian.[5] (Hence, it has been conjectured, a connection with the important family of Asian Hierapolis that produced Antipater the sophist.[6]) The hostility of Philostratus of Lemnos toward Aspasius drew forth a work on how to write letters, a work aimed at Aspasius while he was serving as *ab epistulis graecis*.[7] The biographer Philostratus observed sagely, and with an erudite allusion, that even from an enemy one can derive some positive gain.[8] The eloquence of both Aspasius and his antagonist was improved by mutual censure.

It is with the career of Herodes that documentation of the professional quarrels of sophists becomes more abundant, and problems arise. Herodes' life was full of quarrels. Some of the lesser ones appear in Philostratus—for example, the little war which the young Herodes waged with his low-born teacher Secundus. (Yet when Secundus died, Herodes pronounced the funeral oration and shed some tears.[9]) Philostratus also records

---

[1] *VS*, p. 588.

[2] Ibid. On the use of δημόσιοι ἰατροί in providing professional testimony at trials, see L. Cohn-Haft, *The Public Physicians of Ancient Greece* (1956), p. 71.

[3] *VS*, p. 591.   [4] *VS*, p. 627.   [5] Ibid.

[6] See above, p. 22.   [7] *VS*, p. 628.

[8] Ibid., citing a proverbial notion (cf. Aristoph. *Birds* 375).

[9] *VS*, p. 544. Cf. *Hesperia* 35 (1966), 248–9, from a statue-base; ῥήτ[ορα] Ἡρώδη[ς] ἑαυτο[ῦ φίλον κα]θηγητ[ήν]. The honorand has been identified as Secundus.

the bad relations between Philagrus of Cilicia and Herodes. It was all Philagrus' fault, it appears, for he had a temper he could not control.[1] The incident which Philostratus goes on to describe is full of interest. Philagrus was walking one evening in the Cerameicus with four men 'of the sort that at Athens chase after sophists', an engaging illustration of enthusiasm for sophists.[2] Philagrus, as he was strolling, noticed a young man who seemed to mock him, and he asked his identity. The youth was Amphicles of Chalcis. Amphicles demanded of Philagrus who *he* was, whereupon in rage at not being recognized Philagrus let fall a linguistic barbarism.[3] A charming tale, but there is more. A herm of this Amphicles, evidently set up by Herodes, has been found on Euboea (near Chalcis). There is an epigram of which the speaker is Amphicles himself; he declares that he is sprung from consuls.[4] This revelation is not altogether a surprise in the case of a pupil of Herodes, but for a man mentioned only in the pages of Philostratus it is a welcome supplement to knowledge.

The struggles of Herodes with his Athenian compatriots require a close and lengthy examination. The opposition was led by sophists and others, but the issues were larger than any hitherto adduced. Although there exists considerable evidence for the Athenian opposition to Herodes, there also exists obscurity. The principal sources are Philostratus' biography of Herodes at the beginning of Book Two of the *Lives*, certain letters in the corpus of Fronto, and a selection of Athenian inscriptions. Because of general confusion in modern accounts, prudence counsels first an examination of these sources without prejudice or exploitation.

According to Philostratus, Herodes offended the Athenians by his manipulation of the will of his father, so that they did not receive the annual mina prescribed for each of them.[5] In this context Philostratus alludes unclearly to the role of the freedmen of Herodes' father in the preparation of the will and to Herodes' evil treatment of his own freedmen and slaves.

---

[1] *VS*, p. 578.   [2] Ibid.: οἷοι Ἀθήνησι οἱ τοὺς σοφιστὰς θηρεύοντες.
[3] *VS*, p. 578.
[4] *IG* 12. 9. 1179, part of which is given in *SIG*³ 1240, n. 1. Cf. the discussion of Amphicles by C. P. Jones in *HSCP* 74 (1970).
[5] *VS*, p. 549.

There is mention of Herodes' strong invective against his freedmen.[1] Later Philostratus records charges levelled against Herodes that he had raised his hand against the future emperor Antoninus Pius at the time when Antoninus was proconsul of Asia and Herodes was then in the province. These charges are declared false, because—as Philostratus reasons—there is no reference to them in the attacks made by one Demostratus against Herodes. 'Indeed, Demostratus would not have neglected to describe the incident in his speech against Herodes, when he attacked the man so bitterly that he actually censured those acts of his which are regularly applauded.'[2] Fair reasoning, and Philostratus had more to rely on.

Subsequently Philostratus provides much more about Demostratus' opposition to Herodes. It went back to a quarrel of the sophist with the brothers Quintilii. These two were serving together in some capacity in Greece when Herodes and the brothers, so one tradition maintained, differed over a competition at the time of the Pythian festival. But the truth lay, says Philostratus, in the report that the brothers, invited to a meeting of the ecclesia, were impressed by speeches which denounced Herodes as a tyrant and urged a complaint to the emperor.[3] It has been assumed that one of the Quintilii was praetorian proconsul of Achaea, while the other was legate: hence a date before 151, the year of their joint consulate.[4] After the meeting of the ecclesia which the brothers attended, Herodes' enemies became active, 'men like Demostratus, Praxagoras, and Mamertinus, and many others whose public policy was opposed to Herodes'.[5] Herodes immediately tried to prosecute these people before the proconsul, but they went secretly and appealed to the emperor Marcus, then at Sirmium. Thus, disquietingly, we are now in the year 173 (or possibly 174).[6] Philostratus relates in detail the melodramatic incidents of the

---

[1] *VS*, p. 549.   [2] *VS*, pp. 554–5.   [3] *VS*, p. 559.
[4] P. Graindor, *Un Milliardaire antique: Hérode Atticus et sa famille* (1930), p. 112.
[5] *VS*, p. 559: Δημόστρατοι ἀνέφυσαν καὶ Πραξαγόραι καὶ Μαμερτῖνοι καὶ ἕτεροι πλείους ἐς τὸ ἀντίξοον τῷ ῾Ηρώδῃ πολιτεύοντες.
[6] *VS*, p. 560. Cf. W. Zwikker, *Studien zur Markussäule* (1941), pp. 198–201. *IG* ii/iii². 3606 alludes to Herodes' presence with the emperor in the territory of the Sarmatians.

trial before Marcus; reference is made to Marcus' previous suspicion of Herodes for having shown hospitality to Lucius Verus, presumably as Vedius Antoninus did at Ephesus.[1] We are assured that Herodes was not exiled, despite the asseverations of some that he was. The philosophic emperor solved the problem of punishing Herodes by punishing his freedmen, who were also accused. The punishments were mild.[2] Near the end of his biography, Philostratus comments on the fame and brilliance of Demostratus' speech against Herodes.[3] Once more does Demostratus appear in the *Lives*, this time in connection with the sophist Theodotus, who is said to have collaborated with Demostratus in plotting against Herodes.[4] Such, then, is the testimony of Philostratus, abundant but not wholly clear.

The testimony of Fronto is of much the same quality and no less vexing. One set of letters, at the beginning of Book Three to Marcus Caesar, is concerned with an imminent trial at which Fronto is to speak in denigration of Herodes. Rather surprisingly, Marcus finds it necessary to inform Fronto of an old bond with Herodes, who had been brought up in the house of Calvisius Ruso.[5] The date and circumstances of this trial are equally obscure: Marcus is not yet emperor, but nothing further can be asserted with confidence. Fronto refers to Herodes as an *adversarius* and declares that it will be necessary for him to speak *de hominibus liberis crudeliter verberatis et spoliatis, uno vero etiam occiso; dicendum de filio impio et precum paternarum immemore; saevitia et avaritia exprobranda; carnifex quidam Herodes in hac causa est constituendus*. It is customary to state that Herodes was himself on trial on this occasion and that the date falls between the death of Hadrian and the consulate of Herodes.[6] It is even said that the consulates of Fronto and Herodes in the same year (143) show that their relations have been patched up.[7] Nearly all this is hypothesis. The only certainty here is

---

[1] *VS*, p. 560. For Vedius Antoninus, see above p. 28.
[2] *VS*, p. 561.   [3] *VS*, p. 563.
[4] *VS*, p. 566.
[5] Fronto, *Epist.*, pp. 36–7 van den Hout. P. Calvisius Tullus Ruso, *cos. ord.* 109, was Marcus' maternal grandfather: *PIR²*, C 357.
[6] Fronto, *Epist.*, p. 38 van den Hout. For the date: P. Graindor, op. cit., pp. 76–7; *PIR²*, C 802. Similarly, A. Birley, *Marcus Aurelius* (1966), p. 98: between 140 and 143.
[7] e.g. Birley, op. cit., pp. 103–4. The *terminus ante* of 143 is based on the

that Fronto did take Marcus' advice, for in undoubtedly later letters Herodes appears as a dear friend.[1]

There is still more on Herodes' tribulations in the extant correspondence of Fronto. A Demostratus is mentioned too. Fronto sends to Lucius Verus, absent in the East, a copy of his speech *pro Demostrato* along with a covering letter, and he includes a copy of the covering letter in a communication to Marcus. Remarkably, both letters happen to survive, and so, therefore, do two texts of the letter to Lucius.[2] The date of these letters is about 165, since Fronto complains to Lucius of the deaths of both his grandson and wife.[3] Fronto tells Lucius that he has learned from his brother that a certain Asclepiodotus, censured in the Demostratus speech, is in fact Lucius' friend.[4] This intelligence at first made Fronto consider suppressing the work, but that proved impracticable as it was already too widely disseminated.[5] Fronto says with candour that he will simply make friends with Asclepiodotus, in view of Lucius' regard. After all, Fronto points out, Herodes is now a close friend, *quamquam extet oratio*.[6] What *oratio*? Herodes will have been ill spoken of. It is not absolutely clear from Fronto's Latin whether or not he is referring to the very speech *pro Demostrato*, which he has just been discussing, or to some other. Current dogma on the *pro Demostrato* is that the occasion for the speech was a prosecution of a person called Demostratus by Asclepiodotus at an unknown date and that that Demostratus is different from the antagonist of Herodes in Philostratus.[7] We are not compelled to believe this.

A few further items from Fronto have to be added. In Fronto's letter to Marcus, the Demostratus speech appears in

tenuous argument of R. Hanslik, *Opus. phil. kath. Phil.* 6 (1934), 29 ff. No such *terminus*, in fact, exists.

[1] Fronto, *Epist.*, pp. 106 and 130 van den Hout: *summus nunc meus*.

[2] Ibid.

[3] Cf. Fronto, *Epist.*, pp. 220 ff. van den Hout: *de nepote amisso*. On the deaths of wife and grandson, see A. Birley, *Marcus Aurelius* (1966), p. 192.

[4] Fronto, *Epist.*, pp. 106 and 130 van den Hout.

[5] Ibid.: *Cupivi equidem abolere orationem, sed iam pervaserat in manus plurium quam ut abolere possem*. The text sent to Marcus (p. 106 van den Hout) has *curavi* in place of *cupivi*.

[6] Ibid.

[7] So P. Graindor, op. cit., pp. 78–9, and *PIR²*, C 849 (A. Stein, reversing the opinion he expressed in *P-W* 5. 1. 192).

one instance (in standard modern editions) as *pro Demostrato Petiliano*.[1] This is read in spite of an emphatic warning by an expert that the reading of the Fronto palimpsest at that point is far from certain.[2] In the actual letter to Lucius and in the copy to Marcus there stand only the words *pro Demostrato*.

Finally, the testimony of inscriptions. Paradoxically there is greater clarity here than in the literary evidence. A series of Athenian texts reveals the following facts. An Eleusinian dadouchos of the earlier second century, Ti. Claudius Sospis, had a son Ti. Claudius Demostratus, who served in the mid second century as archon.[3] This Demostratus was married to the daughter of another archon, Aelius Praxagoras.[4] Demostratus' brother, Ti. Claudius Lysiades, was father-in-law of Julius Theodotus the sophist.[5] One may also register in this context the name of another archon of the mid second century, M. Valerius Mamertinus.[6]

Such, then, is the assorted evidence touching the matter of Herodes' Athenian enemies. A few of the more prevalent dogmas of the present time have already been outlined: when combined, they yield a grotesque result.[7] Between 138 and 143 Herodes was prosecuted, Fronto attacking him; Herodes and Fronto are happily reconciled by the year of their consulates. Some time before or in the reign of the *divi fratres* Fronto defends a Demostratus against an Asclepiodotus. Herodes puts up with the existence and circulation of some speech of Fronto, containing unkind remarks about him, but the Demostratus defended has no relation to the known enemy of

---

[1] Fronto, *Epist.*, p. 106 van den Hout. Likewise in Haines's Loeb edition of Fronto, vol. ii, p. 220.

[2] E. Hauler, *Wiener Studien* 28 (1906), 107.

[3] *IG* ii/iii². 2342, l. 21 (Sospis dadouchos); 4071, l. 22 (Demostratus archon). For the relationship, cf. the stemma *ad IG* ii/iii². 3609 and *PIR²*, C 849, with the revisions of J. H. Oliver in his *Athenian Expounders of the Sacred and Ancestral Law* (1950), pp. 80 and 164. See, however, E. Kapetanopoulos, Ἀρχαιολογικὴ Ἐφημερίς 1964 (publ. 1967), 120 ff.

[4] *IG* ii/iii². 2067, l. 2 (Praxagoras archon). Cf. the stemma cited in the foregoing note.

[5] Theodotus: *IG* ii/iii². 3616, 3813, 4087; *VS*, pp. 566–7. Cf. *PIR²*, I 599. It should be noted that the wife of Valerius Apsines, the sophist contemporary with Philostratus (*VS*, p. 628; Suid., s.v. Φρόντων Ἐμισηνός), belonged to the family of Lysiades and Demostratus: *Hesperia* 10 (1941), 261.

[6] *IG* ii/iii². 1773.   [7] Cf. P. Graindor, op. cit.; *PIR²*, C 802 and 849.

Herodes. Some time in the first half of the 170s Demostratus and his allies appeal to Marcus at Sirmium after Herodes has tried to prosecute them in Greece. These events are connected by Philostratus with the presence of the Quintilii brothers in Greece; if one of them is taken to be proconsul, the date is before 151. That means that there were about twenty years between the trouble with the Quintilii and the appeal at Sirmium. Such an interval is the opposite of Philostratus' implication. The whole thing lies in shambles, and it is hardly a trivial topic if it involves Herodes Atticus, not to mention Fronto and emperors.

A fresh interpretation may suitably begin with Demostratus, inasmuch as he (or someone with the same name) appears in each set of testimonies. The Ti. Claudius Demostratus of the inscriptions is certainly identical with Herodes' enemy in Philostratus. Two of the three allies of Demostratus, as specified by Philostratus, turn up as Demostratus' relatives, namely his own father-in-law, Praxagoras, and his brother's son-in-law, Theodotus the sophist. There can be no doubt that Ti. Claudius Demostratus was the man who made his defence before Marcus at Sirmium in about 173.

Now what of Fronto's *pro Demostrato*? One thing is certain; Fronto attacked Herodes only once. Whenever that was, he did it out of ignorance of Marcus' favour of the man; warned, he would not have done it again. Furthermore, it is bizarre to assume that Fronto's Demostratus is not Herodes' enemy, clearly an important person, when Fronto mentions his relations with Herodes in a letter concerned with the Demostratus speech. An assumption of two Demostrati would have to be accepted only if necessitated by Fronto's Latin; in fact, the phrase *quamquam extet oratio* is at the worst ambiguous and—on any less pessimistic view—an allusion to the speech *pro Demostrato*.[1] Therefore, if Fronto's Demostratus is Herodes' enemy, there is no escaping the conclusion that the speech at issue was the very one delivered by Fronto at the so-called trial of Herodes. And yet Demostratus is evidently the defendant.

[1] Of scholars whom I have consulted on this point (they are many), all but one insisted that the natural interpretation is a reference to the *pro Demostrato*. Otherwise, we should expect *oratio illa*, or the like.

The solution is to hand. Herodes' 'trial' was nothing of the sort. It was the trial of Demostratus. In the letters about Fronto's attack on Herodes there is no need for Herodes to be the defendant. Indeed Fronto refers several times to Herodes as his *adversarius*;[1] he is never called a *reus*. Herodes, we may conjecture, was speaking against Demostratus, and he will have been the prosecutor. Fronto was planning some harsh remarks about Herodes to discredit him—perfectly natural court procedure. And he assures Marcus that he will say no more against Herodes than is necessary for the success of his case.[2] There is certainly a correlation between Philostratus' allusions to Herodes' cruel treatment of freedmen and slaves and Fronto's remarks about cruelty and murder;[3] this is doubtless the sort of thing Herodes' enemies brought up. And Fronto's reference to a wicked son unmindful of his father's entreaties is best interpreted as an allusion to Herodes' guile in avoiding the terms of Atticus' will.[4] But the charge could be introduced on any occasion between the failure to execute the will and Herodes' own death. Fronto's remark to Lucius Verus about the circulation of his speech is not helpful in dating what may now be termed Demostratus' trial: we have no knowledge of how many years Fronto required between delivery and publication of a speech, nor can we say how long it took for a work to be so widely disseminated as to become beyond re-claiming. The trial has to have occurred before 161, because Marcus was not yet emperor at the time. There is no other clue. With the certain activity of Demostratus at Sirmium in the 170s, it might be more plausible to locate the trial in the later years of Pius' reign. Whenever it is located, Fronto's surprising ignorance of Marcus' regard for Herodes will be no less surprising. It is easy to over-estimate just how much the fastidious Fronto knew about the personal affairs of the boy he tutored.

The problem of the twenty years intervening between Herodes' quarrel with the Quintilii (and their presence at the

---

[1] Fronto, *Epist.*, p. 36, ll. 18 and 22; p. 38, l. 11 van den Hout. Note also p. 37, l. 24: *mihi cum eo certatio.*

[2] Ibid., p. 38 van den Hout.

[3] *VS*, p. 549 and Fronto, *Epist.*, p. 38 van den Hout (cf. above, p. 95).

[4] Fronto, loc. cit.: *de filio impio et precum paternarum immemore.* Cf. *VS*, p. 549.

assembly) and the appeal at Sirmium can be admirably solved
by assuming the brothers to have been consular *corrector* and
comes.[1] Their presence at the ecclesia may be emphasized:
a proconsul would have no business being there, but a *corrector*
would have been within his rights.[2] Furthermore, a proconsulate of Achaea in this period does not normally lead to a consulate. Hence, two problems are solved at one blow. There is,
therefore, nothing to oppose dating the presence of the Quintilii in Greece to about 171.

The present revised view of the evidence for Herodes'
enemies has some consistency without doing violence to the
sources. To recapitulate: some time under Pius Fronto had
harsh words about Herodes in a speech in support of Ti.
Claudius Demostratus, an Athenian enemy of Herodes, when
Demostratus was on trial. Later, in the early 170s when the
Quintilii brothers were serving as consular *corrector* and *comes*
in Achaea, the troubles for Herodes began which led to the
appeal of Demostratus and his allies (who were in two instances related to him) before the emperor Marcus at Sirmium.
Demostratus' speech attacking Herodes at that time was known
to Philostratus: it was clearly a masterpiece.[3]

After surveying the diverse professional quarrels of the
sophists, one discerns certain features in prominence. The
quarrels at times mirror the factional divisions and political
rivalries within the cities of the East; such were the troubles
that centred upon Herodes at Athens. Other quarrels, like
that of Favorinus and Polemo, bespeak the rivalry of great
cities with each other. But perhaps the most important, certainly the most ominous aspect of the sophists' disputes was the
way in which they could lead to intervention from the appointed magistrates of Rome or from the emperors themselves.
The very eminence of the sophists made this inevitable. There
can be no undervaluing the fact that the Athenian disputes of
Herodes were ultimately settled on the banks of the Danube
by the emperor Marcus.

---

[1] E. Groag, *Die römischen Reichsbeamten von Achaia von Augustus bis auf Diokletian* (1939), pp. 128–31.

[2] Ibid.

[3] *VS*, p. 563: ὁ δὲ λόγος, ὃν διῆλθε πρὸς τὸν Ἡρώδην ὁ Δημόστρατος, ἐν θαυ-
μασίοις δοκεῖ.

VIII

THE CIRCLE OF JULIA DOMNA

WITH all that has been said so far about the sophists of the second and early third centuries and their relations with the Roman government, there has still been no discussion of an aspect of the sophistic revival which has general notoriety among historians of Rome. This is the circle of sophists and philosophers which the empress Julia Domna assembled around her in the reigns of Septimius Severus and Caracalla. Since Philostratus' life and writings have throughout provided an apposite terminus for these inquiries, it is appropriate to turn to a discussion of the coterie to which Philostratus himself belonged. Unfortunately, much of what has to be said on this matter is negative, because for the first time in dealing with the Second Sophistic we touch upon a topic that has been treated often by historians. The result has been a welter of error and misunderstanding. Until recently it has not been the habit of scholars to scrutinize the composition of alleged cultural circles.[1] On the contrary, the custom has been to fill them out with persons not explicitly attested as belonging to them.[2] It will be seen that the circle of Julia will survive scrutiny only at the expense of losing its character and distinction.

The current opinion of Julia and the sophists is remarkably interesting. She gathered around her a group of intellectual luminaries, who satisfied her deep instincts for philosophy and rhetoric. As her origins were in Emesa (in Syria), it is frequently said that there was something eastern about her intellectual leanings, and we are supposed to assume, therefore, that her

---

[1] For a sceptical view of the circle of Scipio Aemilianus, see H. Strasburger, *Hermes* 94 (1966), 60 ff.; cf. A. E. Astin, *Scipio Aemilianus* (1967), pp. 294 ff. For doubts about the circle of Symmachus: Alan Cameron, *CQ* 18 (1968).

[2] Observe the comment of F. Solmsen apropos the circle of Julia Domna: 'Allerdings wird eine gewisse Dosis Phantasie für alle solchen Versuche unentbehrlich sein' (*P–W* 20. 1. 137).

sophists and philosophers were easterners, many Syrian.[1] Scholars have been inclined to make comparison with the Italian princely courts of the Renaissance.[2] One scholar, in a learned article on the Philostrati published in 1907, listed the members of Julia's group: Philostratus the biographer; the lawyers Papinian, Ulpian, and Paulus; the historians Cassius Dio and Marius Maximus; the doctors Serenus Sammonicus and Galen; the poet Oppian, Gordian I, Aspasius of Ravenna, Antipater of Hierapolis, and Aelian.[3] A stunning assemblage. A similar list appeared just over a decade later in a book on Septimius Severus in the English language.[4] Without any documentation the author of that work described Julia vividly, if unedifyingly, as a compound of Catherine de' Medici, Christina of Sweden, and Messalina.[5] There was provided another list of Julia's cultural intimates, which—in addition to duplicating the list of 1907—included Athenaeus the Deipnosophist, Apollonius of Athens, Heracleides of Lycia, Hermocrates of Smyrna, and Alexander of Aphrodisias.[6]

In more recent scholarship the old opinion has been peacefully perpetuated with hardly a trace of critical examination. We have had repeated the comparison with Renaissance courts, and some erudite reflection has been lavished upon the relation between Cassius Dio and Julia.[7] Doctrine about the empress from Syria has persisted (and grown), but no new evidence whatsoever has accrued. In fact, there never has been any evidence for most of what has been written.

[1] For accounts of Julia and her group: K. Münscher, *Philologus*, Suppl. 10 (1907), 477–8; M. Platnauer, *The Life and Reign of the Emperor Lucius Septimius Severus* (1918), pp. 144–5; F. Solmsen, *P-W* 20. 1. 137; E. Kornemann, *Grosse Frauen des Altertums* (1942), p. 267; J. P. V. D. Balsdon, *Roman Women* (1962), p. 152. Especially egregious is the account of J. Bidez in the *Cambridge Ancient History*, xii (1939), pp. 613–14.

[2] Münscher, op. cit., p. 478; Platnauer, op. cit., p. 128. Also cf. Kornemann, op. cit., p. 267: 'Domna erinnert darin an fürstliche Frauen der Renaissance.'

[3] Münscher, op. cit., p. 477.

[4] Platnauer, op. cit., pp. 144–5.

[5] Ibid., p. 128: 'An empress who added the political caprice of a Catherine de' Medici to the intellectualism of a Christina of Sweden and the vices of a Messalina'.

[6] Ibid., pp. 144–5. Cf. Bidez's list in the *Cambridge Ancient History*, loc. cit.

[7] Cf. Balsdon, op. cit., p. 152 (with approval of Platnauer). For the first time, however, a note of scepticism was sounded: F. Millar, *A Study of Cassius Dio* (1964), pp. 19–20, in regard to Dio and Julia.

The whole impressive edifice of conjecture about Julia's circle has a foundation which can be uncovered. In his *Histoire de Rome*, Volume 6 (published in 1879), Victor Duruy first produced the canonical list of the members of the group, and he was the first to compare the court which he had just invented with the courts of the Renaissance (which had doubtless been in his mind from the start).[1] No scholar who has documented his account of Julia has ever referred to anything except Duruy's history or a work which is itself derived from Duruy.[2] The current notion of Julia's circle, therefore, with the list of its members and a nice allusion to Renaissance courts, is nothing more than a nineteenth-century fabrication.

The circle of Julia Domna is attested. That is something. Near the beginning of the work on Apollonius of Tyana, Philostratus says that he had been a member of her κύκλος.[3] In the *Lives* Philostratus notes that Philiscus the Thessalian had also been a member.[4] In Cassius Dio there is one reference to Julia's group, and that is the passage to which we owe our information about its origin: the empress turned to intellectual diversions because of the enmity of the powerful prefect of the guard, Fulvius Plautianus.[5] The κύκλος would appear to have come into being in the late 190s.[6]

It comes as a shock to realize that these few passages from Philostratus and Dio constitute all the certain ancient testimony that exists on the celebrated circle of Julia Domna. From this evidence it may be deduced that there *was* a circle of sophists, philosophers, and the like, that Julia herself enjoyed participating in discussion, and that Philostratus the biographer and Philiscus the sophist were—at least for a time—members

---

[1] V. Duruy, *Histoire de Rome*, vi (1879), pp. 91 ff.

[2] Münscher, op. cit., refers only to Duruy. Platnauer, op. cit., refers to J. Réville, *La Religion à Rome sous les Sévères* (1885): Réville, pp. 200 ff., refers to Duruy. Solmsen, op. cit., refers to Duruy and Réville. Balsdon refers to Platnauer. And so on. Bidez and Kornemann refer to no one.

[3] Philostr. *Vit. Apoll.* I. 3: μετέχοντι δέ μοι τοῦ περὶ αὐτὴν κύκλου—καὶ γὰρ τοὺς ῥητορικοὺς πάντας λόγους ἐπῄνει καὶ ἠσπάζετο κτλ.

[4] *VS*, p. 622 (Philiscus): προσρυεὶς τοῖς περὶ τὴν Ἰουλίαν γεωμέτραις τε καὶ φιλοσόφοις. For an inscription mentioning Philiscus, probably as procurator in Thessaly, see *BCH* 73 (1949), 473, no. 11.

[5] Dio 75. 15. 6–7 (cf. 77. 18. 3).

[6] On Plautianus' rise to power (and fall): *PIR²*, F 554.

of this circle. That is all that can be deduced: no mention of Papinian, Dio himself, Galen, or any other luminaries of the age that have been claimed by modern scholars. Oddly, Philiscus, who really did belong, was consistently omitted by Duruy and his academic posterity.

One further piece of evidence might be introduced by some into this inquiry, namely the letter of Philostratus to Julia Domna.[1] However, it would add nothing at all to the permissible conclusions about the circle—if it were admitted as valid evidence. There is good reason to consider it spurious,[2] and it will be necessary to advance arguments before dismissal.

The letter's object is to demonstrate to the empress that Plato actually admired Gorgias and the sophists; she should not feel that there is incompatibility or animosity between philosophers and sophists. The letter ends with a plea that she persuade Plutarch not to be annoyed with sophists: πεῖθε δὴ καὶ σύ, ὦ βασίλεια, . . . Πλούταρχον μὴ ἄχθεσθαι τοῖς σοφισταῖς. If she fails to persuade him, she in her wisdom will know—the writer assures her—what name, doubtless uncomplimentary, to call him. The conventional interpretation of these last lines of the letter relies upon an appeal to a lost work of Plutarch in which the sophists were attacked. (Such a work certainly did exist.[3]) It is confidently asserted that someone put a copy of Plutarch's denunciation into the hands of the empress and that Philostratus wrote her a letter so that she would not be persuaded by the work.[4] In other words, when the author of the letter says to Julia Domna, 'Persuade Plutarch not to be angry with the sophists', he is really supposed to be saying, 'Do not let Plutarch persuade you to be angry with the sophists.' What is to be done, on this view, with the author's alternative (involving an uncomplimentary epithet) is not easy to divine. It is inescapable that the author of the letter thought that

[1] Philostr. *Epist.* 73.

[2] Apart from W. Schmid, who declared the entire collection of Philostratean letters spurious on stylistic grounds (*Der Atticismus* iv [1896], p. 3), the genuineness of the Letter to Julia in particular has been consistently and stoutly affirmed: Münscher, op. cit., p. 537; E. Norden, *Die antike Kunstprosa* (1915), p. 380; F. Solmsen, *P–W* 20. 1. 165; J. Bidez, op. cit., p. 613.

[3] Cf. Isid. Pel. *Epist.* 2. 42 (Migne, *PG* 78. 484), quoted in Norden, op. cit., p. 380.

[4] Cf. Solmsen, loc. cit.

Plutarch was alive at the same time as Julia Domna and was, moreover, a member of her coterie. If that is the case, the letter is automatically damned.

Besides, there are other reasons for suspecting the letter of Philostratus to Julia. Close parallels can be detected with the biography of Gorgias in the *Lives of the Sophists*. In the letter to Julia two rare technical terms are used to describe aspects of Gorgianic λόγοι: ἀποστάσεις and προσβολαί. These two terms also occur in conjunction in the biography.[1] Reference is made in the letter to the triumph of sophistic rhetoric at Olympic festivals in turning the attention of Greeks to their ancient hostility toward the barbarians; the same point is made in Philostratus' biography of Gorgias, quite naturally there in connection with the famous Olympic oration.[2] Finally, the letter declares that not only was Plato impressed and influenced by the sophists, but no less were Pericles, Critias, and Thucydides; in the biography of Gorgias we read that the great man impressed Critias, Alcibiades, Thucydides, and Pericles.[3] The letter to Julia Domna was evidently written by a person who knew that her circle included both sophists and philosophers, and that Philostratus belonged to it. The biography of Gorgias was accordingly plundered. The author was familiar with a treatise against sophists by Plutarch, but unfortunately—as he must have been writing some long time after—his chronology was bad, converting the sage of Chaeronea into a contemporary of Philostratus. That gives him away.

With the letter to Julia dishonoured, it remains to discover whether any legitimate claim can be made for the dozen or more persons who have been enrolled by modern scholars in the empress's circle. The best case can be made for the Gordian to whom Philostratus dedicates the *Lives of the Sophists*, whichever Gordian that may be.[4] In his dedicatory preface Philostratus recalls a discussion which he and Gordian had held about the sophists when they were in the temple of Apollo at Daphne outside Syrian Antioch.[5] Since one can be certain that

---

[1] *VS*, p. 492.   [2] *VS*, p. 493.   [3] *VS*, pp. 492–3.
[4] On the problem of identifying this Gordian, see pp. 6–8 above.
[5] *VS*, p. 480.

Julia passed the last years of her life at Antioch[1] and since we know that Philostratus anyhow belonged to her circle, it is not an unreasonable inference that Gordian did too. But it is not, of course, a necessary inference; and if the Gordian is the first of that name, we have it from Herodian that he held a great many provincial commands.[2] There is no reason why he should not have been in Syria when Philostratus was there with Julia.

Apart from Gordian none of the other luminaries assigned to Julia's circle has the slightest business being there. It would appear that Duruy and his followers have simply taken note of the most eminent intellectuals of the reigns of Severus and Caracalla and assumed without warrant or argument that they must have been members of the empress's circle. This procedure can yield nothing persuasive: such great figures as Papinian or Antipater were *too* important to waste their time as members of a salon.[3] (This is not to say that they did not exchange an occasional philosophic observation with Julia.) Furthermore, for men of ambition attendance at meetings of Julia's group might not always have seemed the best way to get ahead. It worked for Philiscus, but there is no indication that Julia's patronage assisted any of the other known sophists in their careers. Philostratus, clearly in the circle, got nowhere. He might have hoped to become *ab epistulis* or perhaps professor at Athens. And in the early years of the salon it would have been positively dangerous to belong: we have seen that Julia formed her group to occupy herself in the face of Plautianus' hostility. No ambitious sophist—and any other kind is irrelevant here—would have preferred Julia to Plautianus. Thus, diverse general considerations militate against depositing all known intellectuals of importance in the Severan age in the salon of Julia Domna.

Implausibility is especially apparent with several persons, the doctors for example. Galen died in 199.[4] There was barely time for the old man to settle down to philosophic discussions

---

[1] Cf. *PIR²*, I 663.   [2] Herodian 7. 5. 2.

[3] *HA* Carac. 8. 2 suggests that Papinian and Julia may have been related somehow. This notion has to be rejected: W. Kunkel, *Herkunft und soziale Stellung der römischen Juristen* (1952), pp. 224–9.

[4] Cf. *PIR²*, G 24.

with the empress.[1] Besides, on his past record, it can be assumed that Galen would have taken care to be on good terms with the prefect of the guard, perhaps even to cure him of something.

As for the doctor Serenus Sammonicus, no one who has cheerfully registered him with Julia appears to have noticed that it requires some credulity to believe in his very historical existence. One learned person of that name, flourishing under Marcus and Commodus, is cited in Macrobius, as well as in the Augustan History. We can believe comfortably in *his* existence: he was the author of a work entitled *Res Reconditae*.[2] However, the son of this man is known only from the Augustan History, and not even that untrustworthy work claims him as a doctor.[3] Yet he is often identified with the author of an undated (and undatable) poem of over one thousand lines, commonly called the *Liber Medicinalis*.[4] This specimen of versified medicine (including cures for baldness, dandruff, impotence, and haemorrhoids) appears under the name of one Q. Serenus, who has been installed in many modern handbooks as Q. Serenus Sammonicus, son of the author of the *Res Reconditae*.[5] That son, of course, nowhere appears as Quintus and, as we have seen, nowhere appears at all outside the Augustan History. Further, the doctor-poet is nowhere attested as Sammonicus and is undatable within three centuries. The only things which the poet and the man in the Augustan History have in common is the name Serenus, which is simply not enough.[6] Therefore, not only must we banish the doctor Serenus Sammonicus from the philosophic company of Julia, but we must also banish the medical poet Q. Serenus Sammonicus from history altogether.

[1] This was a difficulty noticed by Bidez in the *Cambridge Ancient History*, xii. 613: '. . . Galen when his great age permitted him to be present'.

[2] Macrob. *Sat.* 3. 9. 6 (mentioning the *Res Reconditae*); 3. 16. 6; *HA* Carac. 4. 4, Geta 5. 5. Servius cites the *Res Reconditae* on *Aen.* 1. 398, 2. 649. Cf. *P–W* II A. 2. 1675.

[3] *HA* Alex. 30. 2, Tres Gord. 18. 2.

[4] Included in Baehrens, *Poetae Latini Minores*, vol. iii. The identification of the two persons is queried in *P–W* II A. 2. 1675.

[5] So in *PIR*, S 123 and in Baehrens's collection of minor poets (cited in the foregoing note).

[6] In fact, the son Serenus Sammonicus is a fiction of the *HA*, which displays other fictitious sons of famous persons; R. Syme, *Ammianus and the Historia Augusta* (1968), p. 186.

The poet Oppian has been regularly lodged in Julia's circle
—often without a hint of the problem of multiple Oppians.
There is no doubt of the distinction between the author of the
Halieutica and the author of the *Cynegetica*; the latter is the one
that has to be claimed for Julia.[1] But there is nothing to support this. The *Cynegetica* is dedicated to Caracalla, and not
unnaturally his mother is mentioned: τὸν μεγάλη μεγάλῳ
φιτύσατο Δόμνα Σεβήρῳ.[2] Is one on the basis of that to put the
author in Julia's circle? Then there are the historians Cassius
Dio and Marius Maximus. No evidence exists for their par-
ticipation in the philosophic conversations, and Dio at least
might have revealed this to us in what survives. Not that we
ought to expect him there anyhow, in view of his attitude
toward philosophers and their associates.[3] In addition, the
remark of Dio's about Julia's low birth is not so uniquely
ungenerous as some may have thought:[4] in another place the
character of Caracalla is derived in part from the evil nature
of his mother.[5] As for Marius Maximus, there is nothing to go
on at all, which makes speculation easier and pointless.

The result of this examination of the evidence for the circle
of Julia Domna is markedly less exciting than the received
accounts. That Julia had a circle of philosophers and sophists
cannot be denied, but apart from Philostratus and Philiscus
its membership is unknown; perhaps a Gordian should be
added. With many great intellectuals in the vicinity of the
court, such as the lawyers who passed to the guard prefecture
or the sophists who became *ab epistulis graecis*, the empress
might have been able at times to engage them in discussion or
to invite them to give a lecture. This would not be unlike the
action of Julia Mamaea, who also had academic pretensions,
in summoning Origen to visit her in Antioch: she had heard so
much about him and was curious to see him.[6] But great and
ambitious men of the age did not settle down to diverting an

---

[1] On the two Oppians, see R. Keydell, *P–W* 18. 1. 698–708.

[2] Opp. *Cyneg.* 1. 4: the antecedent of τὸν is Ἀντωνῖνε in line 3.

[3] For Dio's views on philosophers, cf. F. Millar, *A Study of Cassius Dio* (1964),
pp. 13 and 156.

[4] Dio 78. 24. 1. Cf. Balsdon, *Roman Women* (1962), p. 152.

[5] Dio 77. 10. 2: τὸ πανοῦργον τῆς μητρός.

[6] Euseb. *Hist. Eccl.* 6. 21. 3–4.

empress. Fame and fortune lay more obviously elsewhere. Most of the persons in Julia's κύκλος will have been lesser philosophers and sophists, whose names, if we had them, would be unfamiliar to us. Her philosophers cannot have been much different from those minor practitioners ridiculed by Lucian in his essay on hired philosophers in the houses of the rich and powerful.[1] Such was the circle of Julia Domna.

It might have been thought that the sophists in Julia's entourage provide a fitting culmination to the relations between the sophists and Rome as they developed in the second and early third centuries. This is not so. Yet Julia's sophists are instructive and illustrative, precisely because of the absence of great men. For they were plotting careers in the Roman government, keeping close to the emperor. As the political influence of the empress became greater,[2] they were no doubt pleased to see something more of her. But mobility, geographical and social, was one of the prime features of the Second Sophistic in history. From fame and influence in great cities of the East, like Athens, Smyrna, or Ephesus, the greater sophists passed into the Roman civil service, often by way of prestigious professorships at Athens or Rome. They had more to do than edify an empress.

[1] Lucian, *De mercede conductis potentium familiaribus*.
[2] e.g. under Caracalla.

IX

OTHER LITERARY MEN

IN his biographies of the sophists Philostratus found space for men whom he could not truthfully denominate sophists; yet their achievements were such as to warrant inclusion.[1] The rhetorical prowess of Dio of Prusa and Favorinus the Gaul induced Philostratus to write their biographies. From a historical aspect his decision may be justified no less. The careers of those philosophers and their contacts with the Roman government exhibit, as has already emerged, much in common with the careers and contacts of the greater sophists. It was inevitable that it should be so, for the liaison between politics and literature does not recognize all distinctions in literary activity. If the sophists provide the most illuminating careers for the inspection of a Roman historian, these can nevertheless be paralleled in certain aspects by the careers of other contemporary literary men who belonged to the age of the Second Sophistic but stood apart from the movement itself.

With Dio of Prusa Plutarch can profitably be compared. Both men, offspring of good provincial families, went to Rome as students of rhetoric in the early years of the reign of Vespasian; both men were again in the city under Domitian, and there is reason to think that both, who bitterly hated that emperor, returned to the East without his favour.[2] With their experience of Rome and of Romans, Dio and Plutarch served to instruct the cities of Asia Minor and Greece in the proper conduct of civic affairs within the framework of the Roman

---

[1] *VS*, p. 484. Cf. pp. 10–11 above.
[2] On Dio, see the still authoritative account of J. von Arnim, *Leben und Werke des Dio von Prusa* (1898). On Plutarch, see C. P. Jones, *JRS* 56 (1966), 74 and the forthcoming book by Jones, *Plutarch and Rome*, which will replace the relevant parts of K. Ziegler's article in *P–W* 21; also R. H. Barrow, *Plutarch and his Times* (1967), p. 38.

imperium.[1] Theirs was a valuable, if often frustrating work: what confronted them constantly was the petty factional strife and city rivalry of which the quarrels of sophists were themselves a manifestation. But Dio and Plutarch, unlike the sophists, did not take sides and inflame local sentiment. They tried rather to restore harmony and to encourage a degree of sound, independent local government which would be welcomed by the Roman regime.[2]

From a lofty social and cultural plane Dio and Plutarch addressed themselves, as did the sophists, not merely to the cities and magistrates of the East, but also to the aristocrats and emperors of Rome. Their role in East–West relations at the turn of the century was closely comparable to that of the sophists in the decades following. Dio spoke intimately with the emperor Trajan and proffered philosophic counsel.[3] Plutarch surveyed the battlefield of Bedriacum in the company of L. Mestrius Florus, from whom he received the Roman citizenship;[4] and he presented learned sympotic discussions as well as parallel lives of notable Greeks and Romans to none other than Trajan's marshal (and Pliny's friend), Q. Sosius Senecio.[5] Nor will Plutarch's association with the Avidii be forgotten, for that was a family which produced proconsuls and legates in Greece in successive generations during Plutarch's lifetime.[6] Then there was C. Minicius Fundanus, another friend of Pliny, who went out to govern Asia under Hadrian: some years previously he had received mention from Plutarch in a treatise on spiritual tranquillity, and had appeared as a speaker in a dialogue on controlling one's wrath.[7]

[1] Cf. Plutarch's *Praecepta rei publicae gerendae* and the many admonitory addresses of Dio. On this whole point, cf. G. W. Bowersock, *JRS* 58 (1968), 261 f.

[2] Bowersock, loc. cit. (previous note) and D. Nörr, *Imperium und Polis in der hohen Prinzipatszeit* (1966).

[3] Cf., e.g., *VS*, p. 488.

[4] Plut. *Otho* 14; *SIG*³ 829a (Mestrius Plutarchus).

[5] Cf. C. P. Jones, *JRS* 56 (1966), 67 and 73.

[6] Plutarch and the Avidii: C. P. Jones, op. cit., 71–3, in regard to the *De fraterno amore* and the *Quaestiones convivales*. Cf. the summary account of the Avidii in this period by A. N. Sherwin-White, *The Letters of Pliny* (1966), p. 388. Sherwin-White should not assume, however, that T. Avidius Quietus, suffect consul in 111, was ever proconsul of Achaea.

[7] *De tranquillitate animi* 464 E; cf. *De cohibenda ira*. Fundanus governed Asia in 122/3: Euseb. *Hist. Eccl.* 4. 8. 6.

Like many a sophist later, who eventually took a post in the imperial civil service before his career was done, Plutarch became a procurator under Hadrian. There is explicit ancient testimony on this point and no reason to reject it.[1] Not that Plutarch has to be considered a procurator of any importance in Achaea. His international prestige and influence could not have been made any greater than it already was. The procuratorship will have been an honour, a formalization of a relationship with the Roman government that had long existed.

The two men of letters, Dio and Plutarch, were not, like the sophists, professional world travellers and showmen. Dio, to be sure, wandered much at one time, but from grim necessity and not by profession.[2] Plutarch avowedly preferred his native Chaeronea, from which he seems to have journeyed—in the years of his principal literary productivity—solely to visit his beloved Delphi.[3] But travel was not essential for the political influence of a littérateur. It will be recalled how Aelius Aristides effectively interceded with emperors without leaving Asia Minor.[4] Dio and Plutarch flourished just on the eve of the most colourful period of the Second Sophistic; and although they were not a part of it, their lives adumbrated many of its most pronounced characteristics.

In the age of Polemo and Herodes two historians, whose works have been of great use to modern scholars, may be compared instructively with their sophist contemporaries. These are Appian and Arrian. Information about the career of Appian is not abundant, existing chiefly in his own preface to the Roman history. But the little that is known has a familiar pattern. Appian came from a well-placed family in Egyptian Alexandria, and he did his part for the city until he fled at the time of the Jewish revolt in the last years of Trajan's reign. Subsequently Appian found himself as an advocate in the presence of the emperor; he was on terms with the orator Fronto, and probably thanks to his influence ultimately held

[1] See above, p. 57, n. 6.
[2] Cf. Dio, *Orat.* 36 and 45. 1–2; also 1. 50 and 19. 1–2 on the banishment.
[3] Plut. *Dem.* 2. 2. On Plutarch and Delphi, cf. C. P. Jones, op. cit., 63–6 and Barrow, op. cit., pp. 30–5.
[4] Above, p. 46.

a procuratorship.[1] Once more there appears a well-connected literary man ending up in the civil service.

Flavius Arrianus, from a Bithynian family already possessed of the Roman citizenship,[2] had a senatorial career of distinction. He reached the consulate under Hadrian, waged a campaign against the Alani (about which he later composed a monograph), and governed Cappadocia for a number of years.[3] As a historian of Alexander the Great, Arrian has enjoyed respect to this day; he was equally a philosopher, and it may be noted that his Discourses of Epictetus were dedicated to that eminent aristocrat of Corinth, L. Gellius Menander.[4] The conjunction of philosophy and history recalls the wealthy Pergamene benefactor, A. Claudius Charax, himself a senator and governor of provinces.[5] Further, the sophist P. Anteius Antiochus of Aegae, of whom Philostratus composed a biography, was also a historian.[6] Again and again disciplines intertwine, and throughout is the prospect of public advancement.

Opportunities for historians to make their way in the world were all too numerous. Accounts of Parthian Wars might be profitable at the time of the expedition of Lucius Verus. Many evidently attempted that topic,[7] though achieving considerably less success than Arrian. The cloud of Parthian historians is not very distinct—which may be as well. However, with the Severan age came another major historian, also a senator. That was Cassius Dio, twice consul, governor of Africa, Dalmatia, and Pannonia, companion of Caracalla.[8] He was probably a descendant of Dio of Prusa,[9] and if that is fact we have another instance of literary pursuits passing in a family of means, producing before long a senator and consul. Finally, among historians of the sophistic age, there was also Herodian

---

[1] App. *Prooem.* 15. Against the old view that Appian was *advocatus fisci* at Rome: H.-G. Pflaum, *Les Procurateurs équestres sous le Haut-Empire romain* (1950), pp. 204–5.

[2] The *nomen* puts this beyond doubt.

[3] *PIR*[2], F 219. Cf. G. W. Bowersock, *GRBS* 8 (1967), 280, n. 7.

[4] Bowersock, op. cit., 280.

[5] *Istanbuler Mitteilungen* 9/10 (1959/60) 109 ff.   [6] *PIR*[2], A 730.

[7] Cf. Lucian, *Quomodo historia conscribenda* 14 ff.

[8] F. Millar, *A Study of Cassius Dio* (1964), ch. I.

[9] Ibid., pp. 11–12.

who reveals that his career had embraced both imperial and public magistracies.[1]

A student of the second century who reflects on the intellectual life of that epoch has eventually to reconcile himself to the absence of any reference, however casual, to Lucian in the biographies of Philostratus. Unfortunately the literary bequests of fate do not always coincide with the works of importance thrown up by nature. The fact that a bulk of Lucian's writings survives will not serve to impugn the judgement of Philostratus in neglecting him. Polemo, Herodes, Hadrian the sophist, Damian, for example, have left their traces in many spots, justifying Philostratus' attention to them. There is more warrant for reproaching fate where other evidence is wanting than for reproaching Philostratus for his omissions. Outside Lucian's own works and a wretched derivative notice in a Byzantine lexicon,[2] there is no evidence for Lucian's existence at all. Perhaps Lucian, prolific as he was, was not very important; his Greek and his wit will adequately explain his survival. With that admitted, we may detect other indications that Lucian, in the end, was not a person of consequence.

He appears to have abandoned the practice of rhetoric at the age of forty-two,[3] and there is no sign that he had ever been a rhetorical performer. There is indeed nothing to suggest that he ever ranked (or practised) as a sophist.[4] His own account of a dream in which two allegoric ladies, Sculpture and Education, address him reveals a sharp perception of the influence and worldly success attaching to a career in rhetoric. Reference is made to the patronage of aristocrats and to preferment for public office:[5] as far as can be told, Lucian himself came to enjoy neither of these rewards. He did, to be sure, ultimately join the ranks of those who served the emperor. He became a minor treasury official in Egypt—and was thus obliged to retract his earlier strictures on intellectuals who pandered to the Roman taste for them.[6]

[1] Herodian 1. 2. 5: ἐν βασιλικαῖς καὶ δημοσίαις ὑπηρεσίαις γενόμενος.
[2] Suid., s.v. Λουκιανός.
[3] Lucian, Bis Accusatus 32. The reference is clearly to forensic rhetoric.
[4] Despite J. Schwartz, Biographie de Lucien de Samosate (1965), p. 16: 'il renonça à la sophistique.'   [5] Lucian, Somnium 11.
[6] Lucian, Apologia, with reference back to the De mercede conductis. Lucian's

It is not, therefore, as a sophist in his own right that Lucian merits a historian's scrutiny. It is as a witty and cultivated, occasionally intemperate observer of his own age that Lucian commends himself. His satiric comments confirm the picture of second-century society that emerges with such clarity from the writings of Philostratus and Aristides, or from the inscriptions. The ostentatious grief of Herodes Atticus, attested by Philostratus and Fronto, is confirmed by several passages in Lucian who had, it appears, small liking for the great man.[1] The popularity of the charlatan Alexander of Abonuteichus is fully, though again unsympathetically documented by Lucian, thereby confirming an impression of tastes already generated by evidence for the Asclepius cult.[2] As a formidable Atticist, Lucian was able to make devastating remarks about the linguistic foibles of his time; he has provided historians of literature with inexhaustible material for fashions in Greek at the height of the Greek renaissance.[3]

Some scholars have found in Lucian an enemy of the Roman regime.[4] That was certainly a convenient explanation of his lack of success in its upper-class milieu. But the notion of hostility to Rome has little to recommend it or to support it, and there are few any more to defend it. The more vicious imputations in Lucian, in the *Nigrinus* or the treatise on hired philosophers, are directed either against human weaknesses generally or against men of the East, like himself.[5] Lucian

post in Egypt was evidently that of *archistator praefecti Aegypti*: H.-G. Pflaum, *Mélanges de l'École française de Rome* 71 (1959), 281 ff. J. Schwartz, op. cit., declares on p. 12, 'Aussi n'est-il pas douteux qu'il fut appelé en Égypte par le préfet C. Calvisius Statianus', and he makes much of that supposed fact (and date—between 170 and 175). There is no evidence whatever for the notion. Pflaum, *Les Carrières procuratoriennes équestres* (1961) iii. 1084 registers Lucian duly as in Egypt 'vers 180'.

[1] Lucian, *Demonax* 24, 25, 33. In the *Peregrinus* 19 Lucian was more respectful, if not enthusiastic. Cf. Schwartz, op. cit., pp. 32–3.

[2] Above, pp. 69–71.

[3] Cf. especially the *Lexiphanes*. In general, J. Bompaire, *Lucien écrivain* (1958).

[4] e.g. A. Peretti, *Luciano: Un intellettuale greco contro Roma* (1946), on which see A. Momigliano, *Rivista Storica Italiana* 60 (1948), 430 ff. On Lucian's alleged hostility in general (rejecting the view), J. Palm, *Rom, Römertum und Imperium in der griechischen Literatur der Kaiserzeit* (1959), pp. 44 ff.

[5] Cf. above all Palm, loc. cit. The *Nigrinus*, often invoked, has more to do with Lucian's conversion to philosophy than with Rome. It simply happened

criticized those *Graeculi* who shamelessly exploited to their own profit the tastes of certain Romans. It is important to realize that the barbs of Lucian suggest a genuine annoyance at the right of undeserved success: nowhere in the vast surviving corpus of his writings does he attack sophists such as Polemo, Hadrian, or Damian. The only major sophist he mentions at all is Herodes, and one will not forget that Herodes had many enemies. It could easily have been maintained that his position in the Roman world was undeserved. A perceptive rhetorician turned philosopher is likely to have harboured such an opinion.

Envy was not confined to any one man. The professional quarrels among sophists have already been investigated, but it may be worth noting that charges of deception and fraud, such as that which Lucian levelled against Alexander, can be found elsewhere. For instance, some persons claimed that Dionysius of Miletus had trained his pupils through the use of magic, hence an undeserved reputation in rhetoric.[1] Such an allegation will have emanated from Dionysius' enemies. Philostratus firmly rejected it: 'Who that is enrolled among the wise would be so foolishly careless of his own reputation as to use magic with his own pupils?'[2] Further, when the sophist Hadrian passed away at the age of eighty in high honour, many believed him a magician; that was slanderous, as Philostratus acknowledged.[3] Envious denigration of this kind evokes, above all, the trial of Apuleius before Claudius Maximus, proconsul of Africa, in the year 158/9.[4]

Recipients of honours and objects of abuse, men of letters bestrode the second and early third centuries. Known to each other and known to the Roman government, they entertained multitudes and wielded influence. It is worth noting that men of this kind expressed themselves in prose; the age of the Second Sophistic shows no literary figure of importance, political or otherwise, who was predominantly a poet. The more talented versifiers of the period, men like Mesomedes or Strato, were political nullities.[5] And even their verses acquired

that Nigrinus was living in Rome when he passed certain philosophic comments on humanity.   [1] *VS*, p. 523.   [2] Ibid.   [3] *VS*, p. 590.
  [4] Apul. *Apol.* For the date: R. Syme, *REA* 61 (1959), 310 and 318.
  [5] Mesomedes: in E. Heitsch, *Die griechischen Dichterfragmente der römischen Kaiserzeit i* (1964). Strato: *Anth. Pal.*, Book xii.

something of the frigidity of contemporary rhetoric. It is
symptomatic that Aelius Aristides proclaimed the new poetry
—a poetry in prose.[1] Composing, therefore, in prose, he
fashioned hymns to deities.

In the historical writings of modern times, the era from
Hadrian to Alexander Severus is often presented without
Aristides and the other sophists; or they are registered as an
eccentricity of the age. Far from it: they are possibly its best
representatives. Their families, which had for generations
enriched and benefited the eastern cities, were swallowed up in
the Roman aristocracy, and the arts by which they achieved
their successes reflected and dictated the tastes of an empire.
By the age of the Severi the social and political promise of the
rhetors, in the late Republic and under Augustus, had been
amply fulfilled.

[1] Aristid. 45. 4–13 Keil.

APPENDIX I

THE SILENT SECUNDUS

THANKS to the labours of B. E. Perry we now possess a serviceable volume containing the various versions of the legend of the philosophic but silent Secundus and the replies he is said to have delivered in writing to the questions of the emperor Hadrian. The tale of how Secundus took a vow of silence upon discovering the unchastity of his mother and the scene of his confrontation with Hadrian evidently had a vogue in the Near East: hence versions in Greek, Arabic, Syriac, Armenian, and Aethiopic. What survives is redolent of folk-tale and legend. But there is no reason why there should not have been a real Secundus to whom the fiction should have been attached. Perry (*Secundus the Silent Philosopher* [1964], p. 2) is doubtful that the silent philosopher could be identical with the Secundus in Philostratus' *Lives of the Sophists*, pp. 544–5: 'The only thing that the Secundus mentioned by Philostratus has in common with the subject of our biography is the name and the fact that he was an Athenian.' No, there is something else. Both Secundi flourished under Hadrian. Philostratus' Secundus was a teacher of Herodes Atticus, and Herodes eventually pronounced his old master's funeral oration. There is, however, no mention of silence in Philostratus' brief biography, but that is the basic ingredient of the legendary accretion.

With the silent Secundus the Hadrianic setting must not be forgotten. The Arabic text of the story (§ 9) contains an unnoticed detail, absent from all other versions extant. (It has to be said, unfortunately, that Perry's account of the Arabic version in relation to the other sources is inadequate: cf. R. M. Frank, *Journal of the American Oriental Society* 86 [1966], 347–50.) In the entourage of Hadrian, the Arabic states, there was a certain Salan, the king's cousin: صالان ابن عم الملك. The Aethiopic alludes to this person without naming him. Who is he? Like Secundus or Hadrian himself, he may be a real person. Concealed in Salan, it may be suggested, is none other than *Salinator*, precisely Cn. Pedanius Fuscus Salinator, consul A.D. 118 and husband of Hadrian's niece. (It is worth noting that the horoscope of Salinator survives: *Cat. cod.*

astr. graec. 8. 2. 85 f.) The fact that the Arabic declares the man to be related to the emperor is, with so late and confused a transmission, of far greater moment than the slight muddling of the exact nature of the relationship. We may have in Salan, therefore, further confirmation of the ultimate historicity of the Secundus tale and a welcome detail about a man who tends to disappear from view after his consulate.

APPENDIX II

POLEMO'S JOURNEY WITH HADRIAN

IN the *Physiognomica*, preserved only in an Arabic translation, the sophist Polemo at one point describes in some detail a journey he made in the company of an emperor, indisputably Hadrian. That emperor's high regard for Polemo has long been recognized (cf. above, p. 48); the journey confirms it. The itinerary and date of the visits recorded by Polemo remain in obscurity, chiefly because the evidence itself is so little known that it is little discussed. Some proposals will be offered here in the hope of eventual clarification. The subject requires a knowledge of Arabic, and this may therefore be a suitable place to reiterate an opinion of R. Walzer, *Greek into Arabic* (1962), p. 114: 'Progress has been delayed . . . by the lack of scholars who are used to reading both Greek and Arabic texts and are familiar with textual questions on both sides. Collaboration between classical scholars and orientalists can, in my view, never replace this ambidextrous approach; and it is not surprising that the results of such collaboration have not been encouraging.'

The only accessible text of the *Physiognomica* is that of G. Hoffmann in vol. i of R. Foerster's Teubner edition of the *Scriptores Physiognomici*. The Arabic is full of textual corruptions, as Hoffmann warns his reader in the preface. His Latin translation must not be relied upon as an authoritative rendering of what Polemo wrote, nor can it indicate the possibilities of interpretation or emendation of the Arabic. Although Hugo Jüttner discussed the passage concerning Hadrian's journey (*De Polemonis rhetoris vita operibus arte* [1898], pp. 27–9), he could not do much with its details because of necessary reliance on the Latin translation, which here is gibberish. The passage was again treated, after consultation with orientalists, by A. von Premerstein in his monograph, *Das Attentat der Konsulare auf Hadrian im Jahre 118 n. Chr.*, *Klio*, Beiheft 8 (1908), 47–57. The subject has been neglected since.

In Foerster's Teubner volume (p. 139) the text appears as follows (I have written tā' marbūṭa where it seemed necessary):

فانى صحبت الملك الأكبر مرة فبينما نحن نسير معه من براقة الى أسية ومع
الملك جيوشه ومراكبه فاختلط بهم ذلك الرجل فمررنا على مداين كثيرة حتى
بلغنا البحر فركب الى بون والسروس وبلاد لودية وفروجية ومواضع كثيرة ثم
رجعنا الى آسية على التخريز فى البحر وشرق(؟) الى روكس ثم سار فى السفن
الى انيس

It should have been realized instantly that the meaningless بون
had to be read as يون, i.e. Ionia (cf. يون on p. 127, line 12); and
التخريز, 'strait' (which Hoffmann supposed to be the Bosporus or
Hellespont), makes infinitely more sense if read الجزير, 'islands'.
Fortunately, in preparing his monograph, von Premerstein had the
manuscript re-examined in Leiden by a competent orientalist. It
happened that the correct readings in these two cases were recognized. It can therefore be stated, on the basis of the Arabic text, that
Hadrian, along with Polemo, passed from a certain region (براقة)
to Asia, with troops and chariots (not *naves* as in Hoffmann's
translation) having accompanied them to the sea. The party
visited Ionia, a place called السروس, and parts of Lydia and Phrygia
(these two names are certain in the Arabic). The emperor is then
said to have gone 'to Asia' by way of islands, calling at روكس.
Thence the group went by sea to انيس. The narrative proceeds,
after this, by describing how—in Asia—a man of particularly suspect physiognomy had made an attempt on the emperor's life.

That the journey with Polemo took Hadrian to western Asia
Minor is clear beyond doubt. From what place did he pass over to
Asia? A simple adjustment of براقة produces the answer: ثراقية i.e.
Thrace (cf. ثراقية on p. 111, line 7). That the name was an Arabic
form of Θράκη had indeed been seen by von Premerstein, although
his reading was not quite right. In any event, von Premerstein was
able to operate with a departure from Thrace. He had also perceived what had to be done with روكس, once it was established that
the itinerary at this stage took Hadrian among islands. Read رودس
i.e. Rhodes—another simple emendation.

After so much real progress, it was regrettable that von Premerstein yielded to sheer fantasy in his historical reconstruction of the
circumstances of the journey. The trouble lay in his conviction that
the journey with Polemo could not be identified with any of the
known journeys of Hadrian. Jüttner had argued for Hadrian's visit
to Asia Minor in 123, a date rejected by von Premerstein on the
ground that Hadrian did not arrive by way of Thrace at that time.

Yet the fact is that we do not know by what route he approached
Asia then. All that can be said with confidence is that he went east-
ward after visiting Spain (cf. D. Magie, *Roman Rule in Asia Minor*
[1950], ii. 1470). But von Premerstein was reluctant to date the
journey with Polemo to 123 for another reason too: he assumed the
attempt on Hadrian's life to be identical with the notorious plot of
the four consulars at the beginning of the reign. So strong was von
Premerstein's belief in this identification that he saw no difficulty in
making Hadrian travel in the wrong direction in 118, from west to
east. Passing from Syria to Rome, Hadrian is supposed to have
turned back, after reaching Thrace, for a trip into Asia Minor. Let
anyone credit this who can.

No journey of Hadrian to Asia will fit the evidence of Polemo
apart from that of 123. And one will note *HA* Hadr. 13. 1 on that
journey: *post haec per Asiam et insulas ad Achaiam navigavit et Eleusinia
sacra . . . suscepit, multa in Athenienses contulit . . .* Here are Asia and
islands, precisely as specified by Polemo. There remain in the
Arabic text two further difficulties which can now be resolved both
by conjecture on its own merits and by confirmatory reference to
the *HA*. After visiting Asia and Rhodes, Hadrian went to انيس,
which means nothing. Read as easily اثنس, i.e. (εἰς) Ἀθήνας. That
is intelligible in the context (departure across the Aegean) and
happens also to indicate where Hadrian actually went. Finally: it
has never made any sense for Hadrian to travel *to* Asia (الى أسية)
by way of islands, when he is already *in* Asia. Emend to من أسية
'from Asia'. One may suspect that the reading in the text is
a repetition of the الى أسية a little earlier (at the start of the
journey).

Accordingly, Hadrian and Polemo travelled to Ionia from
Thrace, visited parts of Lydia and Phrygia, then travelled by way
of Rhodes to Athens. However, one place-name in the Arabic is
still unexplained: السروس, evidently in the Ionian vicinity. Von
Premerstein thought that this was Lesbos, but that is wrong because
the hamza cannot thereby be accounted for. It is necessary to read
a definite article before the name. Another simple emendation
solves the riddle: السردس i.e. Sardis. The presence of the definite
article guarantees this reading. In literary Greek there was a strong
tradition of using the article with Σάρδεις. It frequently appears, for
example, in Herodotus (e.g. ἐς τὰς Σάρδις at 1. 35. 1, 43. 3, 48. 1,
etc.) and in Strabo (pp. 625–7 on αἱ Σάρδεις). Polemo, a littérateur
of the second-century renaissance, will have written Σάρδεις with
the definite article, thus leading the Arabic translator to write
السردس.

If the foregoing argument is correct in placing the journey recorded by Polemo in 123, the result has importance. Hadrian travelled to Asia from Spain in that year, not by way of Africa or Crete (as scholars have suggested, cf. Magie, loc. cit.), but by way of the Balkans. Moreover, Sardis and Rhodes are secured for the itinerary.

APPENDIX III

THE DATE OF FRONTO'S DEATH

On the last page of his famous article, 'Die Chronologie der Briefe Frontos', Theodor Mommsen declared that M. Cornelius Fronto (*cos.* 143) must have died in 176 or after: *Hermes* 8 (1874), 216 = *Ges. Schr.* 4. 486. Arthur Stein maintained the same view in *PIR*[2], C 1364. In recent years, however, it has been customary to think that the orator passed away in sadness and infirmity not long after writing the latest securely datable letters that survive, therefore *c.* 166. Grieving over the deaths of both wife and grandson, and himself in ill health, Fronto could not possibly have lasted much longer. So C. R. Haines, *The Letters of Fronto* (Loeb Library, 1919) i, p. xl; H.-G. Pflaum, 'Les correspondants de l'orateur M. Cornelius Fronto de Cirta', *Hommages à J. Bayet* (1964), pp. 544 ff.; A. R. Birley, *Marcus Aurelius* (1966), p. 198, n. 2, where the opinion of Mommsen and Stein is stigmatized as 'an unusually perverse interpretation'. It is time to obliterate this tragic but unjustifiable picture of the end of Fronto. For one thing, any student of the second century A.D. should realize that neither grief nor ill health justifies an inference of imminent decease. Aelius Aristides went on for years and years.

Worse is the inference of decease simply because the correspondence of Fronto, as we have it, appears to break off. A large part of the extant collection is undatable anyway (despite the dangerously beguiling chronology of Haines in the Loeb edition). Furthermore, there is no reason to think that we possess anything like the complete correspondence. The latest researches on the original codex have delivered the conclusion that we now have only 388 pages of a codex that once had 680: M. J. van den Hout, *Cornelii Frontonis Epistulae* (1954), p. xliv. Nearly a hundred years ago Mommsen had similar figures: *Hermes* 8 (1874), 198. No conclusions about the date of Fronto's death ought to have been drawn from the latest datable letter. Indeed, some extant letters may well belong to the period after 166: there is nothing against this.

The opinion of Mommsen and Stein was based on a passage in the *De Orationibus*, addressed to Marcus; and none of those who have rejected the opinion of those scholars has provided an alternative explanation of the text. It reads: *Quid igitur? Non malim mihi nummum Antonini aut Commodi aut Pii?* (p. 154 van den Hout). Fronto is discussing old and new styles in rhetoric, and he has an imaginary interrogator comparing the recent coinage. Now, as Mommsen knew, there was no *nummus Commodi* before the grant of *imperium* to Commodus on 27 November 176. Thus a *terminus post* for the words in Fronto. There is no avoiding this conclusion. It is true that medallions were issued *c.* 166 to commemorate the designation of Commodus and Annius Verus as Caesars (*JRS* 49 [1959], 39 f.), but medallions in bronze are not *nummi*. Besides, Fronto's ordering of the imperial names only makes sense if Marcus and Commodus are understood as the present rulers and Pius as a previous one. And in 166 we should have had the name of Lucius Verus (who, as emperor, is never called Commodus).

One may look more closely for other indications of late date in the extant correspondence of Fronto. There is a letter to Caelius Optatus recommending a pupil, Sardius Saturninus (p. 170 van den Hout): this ought to be addressed to Caelius Optatus as legate of III Augusta in Numidia in 166/7 (cf. *CIL* 8. 2736 and *ILS* 2303, both Lambaesis). Pflaum, op. cit., p. 547, had qualms because Fronto uses the word *frater* to Optatus, and this, Pflaum thought, meant that the Optatus had to be a coeval. That is not necessary; Fronto uses the word to Cornelius Repentinus (p. 180 van den Hout). The Sardius Saturninus recommended to Optatus appears again in Fronto's correspondence (p. 170 van den Hout): Saturninus, in a letter to a Petronius Mamertinus, is seen to have had two sons, one of whom has drowned and the other—another pupil of Fronto—has already embarked on a public career. Manifestly, therefore, this letter is considerably later than the one addressed to Caelius Optatus. And that appeared to belong to *c.* 166/7. The letter to Petronius Mamertinus probably belongs in the 170s somewhere. It may be asked who the recipient should be. Perhaps, M. Petronius Sura Mamertinus, *cos. ord.* 182 and husband of a daughter of the emperor Marcus.

Further, a letter in the collection *ad amicos* (pp. 163–4 van den Hout) is addressed to a certain Claudius Severus. This person is identified by Groag as Cn. Claudius Severus Arabianus, *cos.* 146 (*PIR*[2], C 1027). Fronto's letter implies some kind of judicial activity for Severus. Groag, loc. cit., observed sensibly: 'Quo munere praeditus Severus ius dixerit, nescimus; vide an fuerit praefectus urbi.' Now city prefects normally had iterated consulates (see above, p. 80, n. 3; also Mommsen, *St. R.*[3] ii. 1062): it might be better to identify Fronto's man with Cn. Claudius Severus, *cos.* II in 173 and husband of another daughter of the emperor Marcus. A connection between this Severus and Fronto would hardly be surprising in view of his several contacts with sophists and rhetors (see above, p. 83 on Hadrian the sophist and Galen). A city prefecture for Severus could be fitted comfortably in the vicinity of the city prefecture of C. Aufidius Victorinus, *cos.* II in 183, the son-in-law of Fronto.

BIBLIOGRAPHY

THE following list contains only the more important books and articles cited in the foregoing pages. *P–W* articles are excluded.

VON ARNIM, J., *Leben und Werke des Dio von Prusa* (1898).

ATKINSON, K. M. T., 'The Third Cyrene Edict of Augustus', *Ancient society and institutions: studies pres. to V. Ehrenberg* (1966), 21 ff.

BABELON, E., 'Le Faux-Prophète, Alexandre d'Abonuteichos', *Rev. Num.* 4 (1900), 1 ff.

BACKMANN, P., 'Galens Abhandlung darüber, dass der vorzügliche Arzt Philosoph sein muss', *NGA* 1965, no. 1.

BAGNANI, G., 'Peregrinus Proteus and the Christians', *Historia* 4 (1955), 107 ff.

BALSDON, J. P. V. D., *Roman Women* (1962).

BARIGAZZI, A., *Opere: Favorino di Arelate* (1966).

BARNES, T. D., 'A Note on Polycarp', *JTS* 18 (1967), 433 ff.

—— 'Pre-Decian *Acta Martyrum*', *JTS* 19 (1968), 509 ff.

—— 'Philostratus and Gordian', *Latomus* 27 (1968), 581 ff.

BARROW, R. H., *Plutarch and his Times* (1967).

BEHR, C. A., *Aelius Aristides and the Sacred Tales* (1968).

BENGTSON, H., 'Das Imperium Romanum in griechischer Sicht', *Gymnasium* 71 (1964), 150 ff.

BIRLEY, A. R., 'The Origin of Gordian I', *Britain and Rome: essays pres. to Eric Birley* (1966), 56 ff.

—— *Marcus Aurelius* (1966).

BLEICKEN, J., 'Der Preis des Aelius Aristides auf das römische Weltreich', *NGA* 1966, no. 7.

BLOCH, H., *I Bolli laterizi e la Storia edilizia romana* (1938–9).

BOMPAIRE, J., *Lucien écrivain* (1958).

BORNECQUE, H., *Les Déclamations et les déclamateurs d'après Sénèque le père* (1902).

BOSWINKEL, E., 'La Médecine et les médecins dans les papyrus grecs', *Eos* 48, i (1956; Symbolae Taubenschlag, i), 181 ff.

BOULANGER, A., *Aelius Aristide* (1923).

BOWERSOCK, G. W., *Augustus and the Greek World* (1965).

—— 'A New Inscription of Arrian', *GRBS* 8 (1967), 279 f.

—— 'The Proconsulate of Albus', *HSCP* 72 (1968), 289 ff.

—— Review of D. Nörr, *Imperium und Polis*, *JRS* 58 (1968), 261 f.

BRANDSTÄTTER, C., 'De notionum πολιτικός et σοφιστής usu rhetorico' Leipzig. Stud. z. class. Phil. 15 (1894), 129 ff.

BROCK, M. D., Studies in Fronto and his Age (1911).

BUCKLER, W. H., 'T. Statilius Crito, Traiani Augusti medicus', JÖAI 30 (1937), Beibl. 5 ff.

CASTER, M., Études sur Alexandre ou le Faux-Prophète de Lucien (1938).

CICHORIUS, C., Rom und Mytilene (1888).

—— Römische Studien (1922).

COHN-HAFT, L., The public physicians of Ancient Greece (1956).

DAY, J., An economic history of Athens under Roman domination (1942).

DESSAU, H., 'C. Sallius Aristaenetus', Hermes 25 (1890), 158 ff.

DITTENBERGER, W., 'Athenäus und sein Werk', Apophoreton (1903), 1 ff.

DODDS, E. R., Pagan and Christian in an Age of Anxiety (1965).

DURUY, V., Histoire de Rome, vol. vi (1879).

EDELSTEIN, E. J. and L., Asclepius (1945), 2 vols.

FITZ, J., 'Ummidio Quadrato, governatore della Moesia inferiore', Epigraphica 26 (1964), 45 ff.

FLACELIÈRE, R., 'Inscriptions de Delphes de l'époque impériale', BCH 73 (1949), 464 ff.

FREND, W. H. C., 'The Date of Polycarp's Martyrdom', Oikoumene (1964), 499 ff.

GEAGAN, D. J., The Athenian Constitution after Sulla, Hesperia, Suppl. 12(1967).

GRAINDOR, P., Un Milliardaire antique: Hérode Atticus et sa famille (1930).

GROAG, E., 'Cn. Claudius Severus und der Sophist Hadrian', Wiener Studien 24 (1902), 261 ff.

—— Die römischen Reichsbeamten von Achaia von Augustus bis auf Diokletian (1939).

GRONINGEN, B. A. VAN, 'General Literary Tendencies in the Second Century A.D.', Mnemosyne 18 (1965), 41 ff.

GROSSO, F., 'La Vita di Apollonio di Tiana come fonte storica', Acme 7 (1954), 333 ff.

HANSLIK, R., 'Fronto und Herodes', Opus. Phil. kath. Phil. (Vienna) 6 (1934), 29 ff.

HEPDING, H., "'Ρουφίνιον ἄλσος", Philologus 88 (1933), 90 ff., 241 ff.

HERZOG, R., 'Urkunden zur Hochschulpolitik der römischen Kaiser' Sitzungsberichte d. preuss. Akad. 1935, 967 ff.

HÜTTL, W., Antoninus Pius i (1936), ii (1933).

ISNARDI, M., 'Techne', Parola del Passato 16 (1961), 257 ff.

JAMESON, S., 'Cornutus Tertullus and the Plancii of Perge', JRS 55 (1965), 54 ff.

JEUCKENS, R., Plutarch von Chaeronea und die Rhetorik (1907).

Jones, A. H. M., *The Greek City* (1939).

—— 'The Greeks under the Roman Empire', *Dumbarton Oaks Papers* 17 (1963), 3 ff.

Jones, C. P., 'Towards a Chronology of Plutarch's Works', *JRS* 56 (1966), 61 ff.

—— 'The Teacher of Plutarch', *HSCP* 71 (1967), 205 ff.

—— 'A Friend of Galen', *CQ* 17 (1967), 311 f.

Jüttner, H., *De Polemonis Rhetoris Vita Operibus Arte* (1898).

Kaibel, G., 'Dionysios von Halikarnassos und die Sophistik', *Hermes* 20 (1885), 497 ff.

Kapetanopoulos, E. A., "Ἀναθηματικὴ ἐπιγραφὴ ἐξ Ἐλευσῖνος", Ἀρχ. Ἐφ. 1964, publ. 1967, 120 ff.

Keil, J., 'Vertreter der zweiten Sophistik in Ephesos', *JÖAI* 40 (1953), 5 ff.

Kornemann, E., *Grosse Frauen des Altertums* (1942).

Kunkel, W., *Herkunft und soziale Stellung der römischen Juristen* (1952).

De Lacy, P., 'Galen and the Greek Poets', *GRBS* 7 (1966), 259 ff.

De Leeuw, C. A., *Aelius Aristides als Bron voor de Kennis van zijn Tijd* (1939).

Magie, D., *Roman rule in Asia Minor* (1950), 2 vols.

Marrou, H. I., *Histoire de l'éducation dans l'antiquité* (1960).

Mensching, E., *Favorin von Arelate* (1963).

—— 'Zu Aelius Aristides' 33. Rede', *Mnemosyne* 18 (1965), 57 ff.

Meyer, Th., *Geschichte des römischen Arztestandes* (1952).

Millar, F., *A study of Cassius Dio* (1964).

—— 'Emperors at Work', *JRS* 57 (1967), 9 ff.

Momigliano, A., Review of Peretti, *Luciano*, in *Rivista Storica Italiana* 60 (1948), 430 ff.

Mommsen, Th., 'Die Chronologie der Briefe Frontos', *Hermes* 8 (1874), 198 ff. = *Ges. Schr.* 4. 469 ff.

Münscher, K., 'Die Philostrate', *Philologus*, Suppl. 10 (1905/7), 469 ff.

Neugebauer, O., and van Hoesen, H. B., *Greek Horoscopes* (1959).

Nock, A. D., 'Alexander of Abonuteichos', *CQ* 22 (1928), 160 ff.

Norden, E., *Die antike Kunstprosa* (1915).

Nörr, D., *Imperium und Polis in der hohen Prinzipatszeit* (1966).

Oliver, J. H., 'Two Athenian Poets', *Hesperia*, Supp. 8 (1949), 243 ff.

—— *The Athenian expounders of the sacred and ancestral law* (1950).

—— *The ruling power* (1953).

—— 'The Sacred Gerousia and the Emperor's Consilium', *Hesperia* 36 (1967), 329 ff.

—— *The civilizing power* (1968).

—— 'The Ancestry of Gordian I', *AJP* 89 (1968), 345 ff.

130   BIBLIOGRAPHY

PACK, R., 'Two Sophists and Two Emperors', *CP* 42 (1947), 17 ff.

PALM, J., *Rom, Römertum, und Imperium in der griechischen Literatur der Kaiserzeit* (1959).

PERETTI, A., *Luciano: Un intellettuale greco contro Roma* (1946).

PERRY, B. E., *Secundus the silent philosopher* (1964).

PETERSEN, L., 'Iulius Iulianus, Statthalter von Arabien', *Klio* 48 (1967), 159 ff.

PFLAUM, H.-G., *Les Procurateurs équestres sous le Haut-Empire romain* (1950).

—— 'Lucien de Samosate, *Archistator praefecti Aegypti*', *Mélanges de l'École française de Rome* 71 (1959), 281 ff.

—— *Les Carrières procuratoriennes équestres* (1960–1), 4 vols.

—— 'Les Correspondants de l'orateur M. Cornelius Fronto de Cirta', *Hommages Bayet* (1964), 544 ff.

—— 'Le Règlement successoral d'Hadrien', *Historia-Augusta Colloquium Bonn 1963* (1964), 91 ff.

PLATNAUER, M., *The life and reign of the Emperor Lucius Septimius Severus* (1918).

POHL, R., *De graecorum medicis publicis* (1905).

POUILLOUX, J., 'Une famille de sophistes thessaliens à Delphes au IIe s. ap. J.-C.', *REG* 80 (1967), 379 ff.

VON PREMERSTEIN, A., *Das Attentat der Konsulare auf Hadrian, Klio*, Beiheft 8 (1908).

REIDINGER, W., *Die Statthalter des ungeteilten Pannonien und Oberpannoniens* (1956).

REINMUTH, O., 'A working list of the Prefects of Egypt 30 B.C.–A.D. 299', *Bulletin of the American Society of Papyrologists* 4 (1967), 75 ff.

RÉVILLE, J., *La Religion à Rome sous les Sévères* (1885).

ROBERT, L., *Les Gladiateurs dans l'orient grec* (1940).

—— *La Carie* ii (1954).

—— 'Inscriptions d'Aphrodisias', *Ant. Class.* 35 (1966), 377 ff.

ROHDE, E., 'Γέγονε in den Biographica des Suidas', *Rh. Mus.* 33 (1878), 161 ff., 638 ff.

—— 'Die asianische Rhetorik und die zweite Sophistik', *Rh. Mus.* 41 (1886), 170 ff. = *Kl. Schr.* 2 (1901), 75 ff.

—— *Der griechische Roman* (1914).

SARIKAKIS, Th., *The hoplite general in Athens* (1951).

—— "Αἱ ἐπὶ τοῦ ἐπισιτισμοῦ τῶν Ἀθηνῶν ἁρμοδιότητες τοῦ στρατηγοῦ ἐπὶ τὰ ὅπλα", *Platon* 9 (1957), 121 ff.

SARTON, G., *Galen of Pergamum* (1954).

SCHISSEL, O., 'Lollianos aus Ephesos', *Philologus* 82 (1927), 181 ff.

—— 'Die Familie des Minukianos', *Klio* 21 (1926), 361 ff.

SCHMID, W., *Der Atticismus* iv (1896).

SCHWARTZ, J., *Biographie de Lucien de Samosate* (1965).

SHERWIN-WHITE, A. N., *The Letters of Pliny: A social and historical commentary* (1966).

SOLMSEN, F., 'Some Works of Philostratus the Elder', *TAPA* 71 (1940), 556 ff.

STEIN, A., 'Zu Lukians Alexandros', *Strena Buliciana* (1924), 257 ff.

—— 'Zur sozialen Stellung der provinzialen Oberpriester', *Epitymbion Swoboda* (1927), 300 ff.

—— *Die Präfekten von Aegypten* (1950).

STEMPLINGER, E., *Strabons literarhistorische Notizen* (1894).

SYME, R., 'Antonine Relatives: Ceionii and Vettuleni', *Athenaeum* 35 (1957), 306 ff.

—— *Tacitus* (1958), 2 vols.

—— 'Hadrian the Intellectual', *Les Empereurs romains d'Espagne* (1965), 243 ff.

—— 'The Ummidii', *Historia* 17 (1968), 72 ff.

—— *Ammianus and the Historia Augusta* (1968).

THOMASSON, B., *Die Statthalter der römischen Provinzen Nordafrikas von Augustus bis Diokletianus* (1960), 2 vols.

THOMPSON, H. A., 'The Odeion in the Athenian Agora', *Hesperia* 19 (1950), 31 ff.

TOD, M. N., 'Sidelights on Greek Philosophers', *JHS* 77 (1957), 132 ff.

TOWNEND, G. B., 'The Post *Ab Epistulis* in the Second Century', *Historia* 10 (1961), 375 ff.

WADDINGTON, W. H., *Mémoire sur la chronologie de la vie du rhéteur Aelius Aristide* (1867).

WALDEN, J., *The universities of ancient Greece* (1912).

WELLES, C. B., 'The Romanization of the Greek East', *Bulletin of the American Society of Papyrologists* 2 (1965), 75 ff.

WILAMOWITZ-MOELLENDORFF, U. VON, 'Asianismus und Atticismus', *Hermes* 35 (1900), 1 ff.

—— Review of Boulanger, *Aristide*, in *Litteris* 2 (1925), 125 ff.

—— 'Der Rhetor Aristides', *Sitzungsberichte Akad. Berlin* 1925, 333 ff.

—— 'Marcellus von Side', *Sitzungsberichte Akad. Berlin* 1928, 3 ff.

WIRTH, G., "Ἀρριανὸς ὁ φιλόσοφος", *Klio* 41 (1963), 221 ff.

—— 'Helikonios der Sophist', *Historia* 13 (1964), 506 ff.

WOOD, J. T., *Discoveries at Ephesus* (1877).

WOODHEAD, A. G., 'The State Health Service in Ancient Greece', *Cambridge Historical Journal* 10 (1952), 235 ff.

ZWIKKER, W., *Studien zur Markussäule* (1941).

INDEX

The following index is envisaged as an integral part of the book. It contains, in some cases, information not to be found in the text or notes. Notably, wherever possible, the full Roman names of the sophists are provided. Sophists and other literary persons, as well as emperors, have been indexed under their familiar names; other Romans will be located by their *gentilicia*. All dates are A.D. unless otherwise indicated. In references to successive pages, the appearance of the rule implies a more or less continuous discussion; the enumeration of individual pages in succession indicates isolated references.

K

Elegeia, 71, 87.
Elpinice, Herodes' daughter, 7 n.
Emesa, in Syria, 5, 21, 101.
Ephesus, 4, 12 n., 22, 30, 43, 52, 54, 56, 63, 78, 95; major centre of rhetoric, 17–18, 19 n., 109; statues and buildings in, 17–18, 27–8; rivalry with Smyrna, 45–7, 90–1.
Epictetus, Stoic, 51 n., 113.
Sex. Erucius Clarus (cos. II, 146), 80 n.
Erythrae, 6.
Euboea, 93.
Eucles, son of Herod of Marathon, 23 n.
Eudemus, great-great-grandfather of Dexippus, 24 n.
Eudemus, Peripatetic, 60 n., 62.
Euodianus, sophist, 24.
Eupolis, 69.
Euripides, 59.
Eusebius, 4 n., 83.

Favorinus, of Arelate, 11, 15, 21, 53, 73 n., 84, 110; immunity case, 35–6, 41–2; rivalry with Polemo, 90–1, 92, 100; exile, 36, 51–2, 81.
Flavii Menandri, of Ephesus, 4 n., 24, 26.
T. Flavius Alexander, of Thessaly, 4 n.
M. Flavius Antonius Lysimachus, of Aphrodisias, 21 n.
Flavius Archippus, of Prusias, 33.
Flavius Boëthus, consular, 62, 63.
Flavius Damianus, consular son of a sophist, 28 n.
T. Flavius Glaucus, 11, 24.
Flavius Phaedrus, consular son of a sophist, 28 n.
T. Flavius Vedius Antoninus, consular son of a sophist, 28 n.
Fronto, of Emesa, 5, 21 n.
C. Fulvius Plautianus (cos. II, 203), 12, 103, 106.

Gadara, 5, 21.
Galatia, 21, 56.
Galen: Aelius Galenus, 12–13, 25, 58–75, 82–4, 86, 102, 104, 106–7, 126.
Gaul, 15.

L. Gavius Clarus, of Attaleia, 81.
Aulus Gellius, 79, 81.
L. Gellius Menander, of Corinth, 113.
Germany, Lower, 79.
Geta, 53, 56.
Gibbon, Edward, 75.
Glabrio, the person in Aristides, 37, 39. See M'. Acilius Glabrio.
Gladiators, 62.
Glaucus, Plutarchean interlocutor, 67.
Glycon, snake deity, 71, 87.
Gordian, honorand of the VS, 5–8, 10, 105, 106, 108. See Gordian I and Gordian II.
Gordian I, the Emperor, 6–8, 102.
Gordian II, 7–8.
Gorgias, 2, 8, 104, 105.
Greece, 15, 17, 29, 89. See Achaea.
Groag, Edmund, 78.

Hadrian, the Emperor, 15, 47, 80 n., 83, 111; and immunities, 32, 34–6, 39, 41–2, 66; and Polemo, 18, 45, 48–9, 120–3; and Herodes, 58; and Marcus of Byzantium, 20, 46; and Heliodorus and Eudaemon, 50–2; and Dionysius of Miletus and Favorinus, 51–3, 81, 90; and Plutarch, 112.
Hadrian, of Tyre, 12, 13, 21 n., 41, 55, 63, 72, 82–4, 91–2, 114, 116, 126.
Hadrianoutherai, 18, 26, 38.
Healing, divine, 70.
Heliodorus, of Arabia, 21 n., 46, 57.
Heraclea, Pontic, 67, 91.
Heraclea, Salbacensis, 65.
Heracleides, of Lycia, 22, 26, 27, 40, 90, 102.
P. Herennius Ptolemaeus, 24.
Hermocrates, of Phocaea: L. Flavius Hermocrates, 24, 27, 48, 73 n., Hermogenes, of Tarsus, 21 n., 89.
Herodes, of Marathon, 23 n.
Herodes Atticus: L. Vibullius Hipparchus Ti. Claudius Atticus Herodes (cos. 143), 3, 4, 7, 16, 17, 18, 20, 25, 28, 48, 56, 58, 74, 86, 88, 114, 116, 118; ancestry, 22–3; benefactions, 27, 29; enemies, 87, 89, 92–100; friends, 49, 78–9,

PRINTED IN GREAT BRITAIN
AT THE UNIVERSITY PRESS, OXFORD
BY VIVIAN RIDLER
PRINTER TO THE UNIVERSITY

Date Due